Richard Deacon's
MICROWAVE COOKERY

CONTENTS

ANOTHER BEST-SELLING COOKERY VOLUME FROM
HPBOOKS

Publishers: Mary Powers, Helen Fisher; Editor: Carlene Tejada; Recipes developed and tested by Richard Deacon, Teri Jewell, Janice Duff, Barbara Dingfelder, Madeline Brown, Michael Snyder; Consultant: Lorine Craft; Food Stylist: Mable Hoffman; Editor-in-Chief: Carl Shipman; Art Director: Josh Young; Book Design: Don Burton; Typography: Frances Ruiz, Cindy Coatsworth; Food Photography: George de Gennaro Studios.

Published by HPBooks, P.O. Box 5367, Tucson, Arizona 85703
Co-Publisher, Thermador, 5119 District Blvd., Los Angeles, California 90040

ISBN: Softcover 0-912656-73-5 Hardcover 0-912656-74-3 HPBook Number: Softcover 73 Hardcover 74
Library of Congress Catalog Card Number: 77-73892 ©1977, Printed in U.S.A. 5-77

Richard Deacon

IF YOU'VE NEVER USED A MICROWAVE OVEN . . .

Let us show you all the advantages and techniques of this wonderful appliance. We want *Microwave Cookery* to live up to all your expectations. We know how anxious you are to begin, so why not take a coffee break and read on. You will be a pro in no time!

TO MAKE A CUP OF COFFEE, TEA OR SOUP

Fill your favorite mug with water. Be sure the mug has no gold or silver trim or metallic glazes on it.

Place the mug on the shelf and close the door.

Push High and set timer for 1-1/2 to 2-1/2 minutes.

When the timer finishes ringing, open the door and remove the mug; the handle will be cool enough to hold.

Add instant coffee, your favorite tea or instant soup and stir. Perked coffee that is cold can be reheated the same way and won't become stronger.

PRECAUTIONS TO AVOID POSSIBLE EXPOSURE TO EXCESSIVE MICROWAVE ENERGY

Do not attempt to operate this oven with the door open since open-door operation can result in harmful exposure to microwave energy. It is important not to defeat or tamper with the safety interlocks.

Do not place any object between the oven front face and the door or allow soil or cleaner residue to accumulate on sealing surfaces.

Do not operate the oven if it is damaged. It is particularly important that the oven door close properly and that there is no damage to the: (1) door (bent), (2) hinges and latches (broken or loosened), (3) door seals and sealing surfaces.

The oven should not be adjusted or repaired by anyone except properly qualified service personnel.

Let's "Think Microwave"

BRIDGING THE GAP FROM CONVENTIONAL COOKING TO MICROWAVE COOKING

This cookbook was written as a guide to help you understand how your microwave oven cooks food. The more you understand this process, the more success you'll have with the foods you cook in it.

It took time for you to learn to cook conventionally. In the beginning you relied on cookbooks and the help of a friend, possibly. Now you're familiar with the techniques and times, so cooking conventionally just comes naturally. You seldom refer to a recipe unless you want to try something new. Then you may check out several cookbook sources before deciding on the final recipe to use.

Microwave cooking is a new form of cooking and requires new techniques. However, much of what you already know about conventional cooking will help you to understand your microwave oven.

You put a recipe together differently. There are tips to learn about microwave cooking just as there were tips to learn about conventional cooking. Learning these tips takes time and practice and talking about microwave cooking with your friends. You'll pick up lots of hints from others

about recipes and ways of preparing food in your microwave oven just as you've picked up ideas about conventional recipes in the past.

We hope this cookbook will help you learn about microwave cooking. Take the time to learn, and "thinking microwave" will come as natural to you as "thinking conventionally" does now.

Microwave ovens come in several styles, from several manufacturers. They all use the magic of microwaves. This book was prepared through cooperation with the makers of Thermatronic Microwave Ovens and all recipes have been tested in Thermatronic Microwave Ovens.

Users of any brand can share and enjoy these recipes. Minor adjustments in cooking time may be required and the information you need is on pages 18 and 19. Before you use any brand of microwave oven, be sure to read the instructions carefully and pay particular attention to the advice on use of metal. Some brands can use metal food-containers with certain restrictions; others tolerate no metal at all in the oven. Whatever your brand, be sure to follow the instructions that come with your oven. Failure to do that may be an expensive mistake, resulting in damage.

How Microwave Ovens Work

Microwaves are high-frequency radio waves. They are generated by an electronic tube called a *magnetron*, just as though you had a miniature broadcasting station in your oven.

From the magnetron, microwaves enter through openings in the top of the cooking cavity. They heat the food you put in the oven. To get uniform heating, the microwaves must be uniformly distributed in the oven. Thermatronic ovens do this by a stirrer, with blades, in the top of the oven. This stirrer scatters the microwaves evenly throughout the oven.

Microwaves have three characteristics you should know. They are *reflected* by metals—therefore they can't get inside a metal container to heat food. They *pass through* non-metals, usually without heating the non-metallic container. Thus you can heat a cup of coffee without getting the cup itself very hot. They are *absorbed* by moisture and this produces heat. It's the moisture in food that is heated by microwaves, so there must be some moisture present to produce heat.

When absorbing microwave energy, the molecules of water vibrate against each other rapidly. This causes friction which produces heat. If you rub your hands together rapidly, you feel heat. This is what happens inside food in a microwave oven.

The assigned operating frequency of Thermatronic microwave ovens is 2450 megahertz. That means the vibrations that cause friction to heat the food occur 2,450,000,000 times each second.

Because microwaves can't pass through metal, they are confined inside the oven. You may see light around the edge of the door. This is normal and you don't need to worry about it. Microwaves cannot pass through even though light does. The oven door is provided with a seal which keeps microwave energy inside the oven. A metal screen between the inner and outer glass door panels is specially designed to prevent the passage of microwave energy.

Your oven should be plugged into an electric circuit without other appliances connected to the same circuit. Too many appliances on the same circuit may overload the circuit and trip the household breaker. Long extension cords will tend to slow down the cooking speed.

Also, be sure the unit is properly grounded as discussed in the instructions that come with the oven.

PLAY IT COOL

Even though microwaves heat the food first, containers can get hot. Here are some tips to observe:

As the food heats, it transfers its heat to the container. When you remove a dish from the microwave oven, it will be hottest where the food touches the container. It may be hot everywhere because heat spreads in the container.

A pie crust touches the entire container so you must use pot holders to remove it from the oven—it will be hot everywhere. The handles of a casserole dish will be cooler than the dish itself, but may still be too hot to touch. If you are steaming something for a long period, steam carries heat and the entire container may be hot.

There's an electric heating element in the top of the oven, used sometimes for browning food. If it has been turned on, be careful not to touch containers with your bare hands. The heat from an electric element heats everything, including the containers and the oven walls.

Be safe. Check dishes and handles before grasping them tightly. Hold your hand nearby, or touch a surface quickly and lightly with your finger. If it is hot, you will know it without getting burned. To be sure, always use a pot holder.

Be very careful about small pieces of metal. If placed in a microwave oven, they may absorb enough energy to become very hot. Avoid using twist-ties made of metal; remove metal staples if present; check food packaging carefully.

How To Cook in Your Microwave Oven

Cooking in your microwave oven is very similar to the conventional way. You can bake, roast, stew, steam, poach, boil, sauté and grill foods in your microwave oven. You'll find when conventional recipes call for a double-boiler, you can cook successfully, with no scorching or lumping, and without that second container of water. However, the techniques for doing these things in your microwave oven differ from the conventional methods.

A microwave oven requires no preheating. You can cook frozen convenience foods without defrosting them first. In fact, many cooks use their microwave ovens only for heating frozen convenience foods and heating leftovers. But the microwave can do so much more.

It does a superb job of cooking many foods from "scratch." Microwave-cooked fresh vegetables are beautiful and retain their garden color and flavor because they are cooked with very little water. Most casseroles can be cooked in about 20 minutes. Your microwave oven is great for defrosting meats and other foods. If friends drop in unexpectedly, you can still serve a delicious meal—even if it means defrosting the roast.

This popular Thermatronic Microwave Oven has three power levels and other capabilities including Browner and Stay Hot. Timer is the large illuminated dial below the control buttons.

LOW — MEDIUM — HIGH

There are five buttons across the top of some control panels: OFF, LOW, MEDIUM, HIGH and BROWN.

LOW, MEDIUM and HIGH control how fast the food is cooked. Some foods, because of their delicate make-up, need to be cooked slowly to avoid toughening. These foods use MEDIUM or LOW. Ovens with only one cooking speed are always on the HIGH setting.

Selecting the correct power level and time is very important in microwave cooking.

A good indication of the microwave power level at each control setting is the electrical power used. Cooking power is measured in Watts. For Thermatronic ovens, the power ratings are:

High:	650 Watts
Medium:	485 Watts
Low:	320 Watts

Other brands may use more or less power at each control setting. If so, cooking will be a little slower or faster. To adjust cooking time, see pages 18 and 19.

These Foods Cook Best at the Indicated Temperatures

HIGH	MEDIUM	LOW
Liquids	Pie crust	Yeast breads
Puddings	Poultry	Eggs
Sauces	Cakes	Cheese
Soups	Roasts, small	Soufflés
Some meats	Defrost frozen	Pot roasts
Fish	*cooked* foods	Roasts, large
Cereals		Melting butter
Vegetables		Melting chocolate
		Defrost frozen
		uncooked foods

THE BROWNER ELEMENT

The Browner is an electric heating element at the top of the oven. It is used for foods that are conventionally browned in an oven. To operate, simply press the Browner button as directed in the recipe and set the timer as required, depending on the type of food. This is especially helpful for foods that are in the oven for a short time and do not have much exterior fat. For example, pie crusts, meringues, bar cookies, cobblers, poultry, crumb toppings, meat loaf, chops, soufflés and appetizers.

A large piece of meat with exterior fat will brown in the microwave oven because of the length of time it's in the oven. You may still wish to brown it more with the Browner.

The Browner does a great job of giving foods eye appeal; it also adds texture to some foods. Microwave cooking retains so much of the original moisture that some foods don't develop the desired texture. Pie crusts and crumb toppings cook well in the microwave oven, but are colorless and don't have the familiar texture you expect. As the Browner is browning these, it's also gently drying them out. Pie crust becomes flaky and crumb topping becomes crunchy.

The Browner is also used to finish some recipes. Although the browner element is intended for browning, not cooking, it *is* capable of finishing-off recipes to perfection.

Turn on the Browner for a few minutes. Its radiant heat gently dries moist areas as the food browns. The finished product is perfect.

Some models of Thermador Microwave Ovens operate on 120/240-Volt circuits. These models can use the Browner while cooking with microwaves. Thermatronic ovens that operate on 120-Volt circuits do not brown and cook simultaneously. Browning is done after or before cooking. These models are designed so you cannot depress a microwave power-level button and the Brown button simultaneously.

STAY HOT

The STAY HOT button turns your Thermatronic microwave oven into a warming oven which can keep food either moist or crisp. It uses the same electric-heating element as the Browner, but the element cycles on and off to maintain approximately a 150°F (66°C) temperature.

To keep foods hot yet moist, they should be covered. Because heat from the electric element is radiant heat, don't cover with plastic wrap. It will melt. Use a glass lid or aluminum foil. Remember to use pot holders when handling items from the Stay Hot.

Foods will crisp if left uncovered. Put food to crisp on the metal rack in a utility dish to heat first by microwave. Then crisp it under the Stay Hot for 10 to 15 minutes. The metal rack allows dry air to circulate around the food.

Foods can be kept hot for 1 to 2 hours under the Stay Hot *without* continuing to cook. It is radiant heat, not microwave power.

Pressing the Stay-Hot button when you begin to cook causes it to come on automatically at the end of the microwave cooking process. If you want to pick up your children at 4:00, run some errands, and have dinner ready to serve when you get home at 6:00, use the Stay-Hot feature. Just select the cooking power, set the timer for the length of time you want to cook, press the Stay-Hot button and your dinner will be piping hot and ready to serve when you return home.

Stay Hot is an unique feature of Thermador-brand microwave ovens.

SHELF POSITIONS

Most microwave ovens have a shelf that can be placed in two positions. Food is usually cooked with the shelf in the lower position unless a recipe states otherwise. This lower position is about 1 inch above the bottom of the oven. DO NOT PLACE THE SHELF OR COOKING UTENSILS ON THE BOTTOM OF THE OVEN because then microwaves cannot pass through the bottom of the cooking utensil and food will be undercooked on the bottom.

When a recipe says, "Lower shelf," this means to position the shelf in its lower position. When a recipe says, "Raise shelf," this means put the shelf in its upper position. The upper-shelf position is used for browning food with the Browner when the food and utensil will fit with the shelf raised. The upper position is also used with some recipes to ensure thorough cooking of food on the bottom of the container.

USING A BROWNING DISH

Some foods, such as steaks and grilled-cheese sandwiches, require direct contact with a hot surface to brown properly. These are conventionally cooked on a grill or in a skillet. With many brands of microwave ovens, including Thermatronic, you can use a special browning dish to do the same thing. These dishes are made of a material that absorbs the microwave energy and therefore the bottom of the dish itself gets hot. Check your dealer for availability of browning dishes.

These are preheated by putting them into the microwave oven. The food to be browned is then placed in the hot browning dish.

When you remove the hot browning dish from the oven, place on a heatproof trivet or asbestos pad. Don't put it on any surface that could be damaged by heat. Don't place a hot browning dish on paper or plastic because these materials may burn.

Instructions for use of browning dishes are included with the utensil.

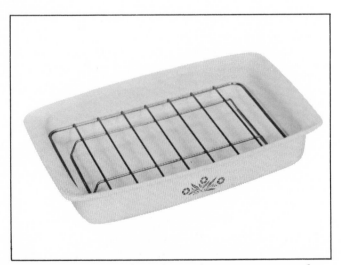

This handy Utility Dish can be used to prepare many of the recipes in this book.

Utensils

In your microwave oven, you can cook and reheat in ways you never dreamed possible. Imagine heating and serving food on paper plates or napkins!

Use of Metals—Do not use metal pots and pans. Microwaves don't pass through metal, so food in a metal container will not cook. Some brands of microwave ovens may be damaged by use of metal utensils. Small pieces of metal may become very hot. Refer to manufacturer's Users Manual for specific instructions as to the use of metal.

You Can Use Things You Already Own—You don't need special utensils. Your kitchen is full of things suitable for use in a microwave. If you are just stocking your kitchen, a good starter-set is: a 4-quart covered-casserole, a 2-quart covered-casserole, a utility dish with a metal rack for meats and several heat-resistant-glass measuring cups from 2-cup to 8-cup size.

How To Test Utensils—A utensil you are not sure about can be tested easily. Put the empty non-metallic utensil in your microwave and set the power on High for 30 seconds. If the utensil remains cool, it's perfect. If it becomes lukewarm, you may use it to warm foods that are already cooked. If it becomes warm or hot, it is *not* suitable. This indicates that the utensil is absorbing microwaves and will get hot during cooking. Then the food won't cook properly. Repeated use of an unsuitable utensil can damage both the oven and the utensil.

How To Choose Utensils—When you select a utensil, consider material, shape and size. Choose a shape that is longer and wider than it is deep. Liquids require a container that is twice the height of the liquid. This reduces the chance of boiling over. Improper shape and size can affect both cooking time and appearance of the finished product. Too large a utensil results in overcooked edges and an undercooked center. Too small a utensil results in longer cooking time and the food will need more stirring and attention. It's best to use the utensil size suggested in the recipes in this book.

Microwave Yes

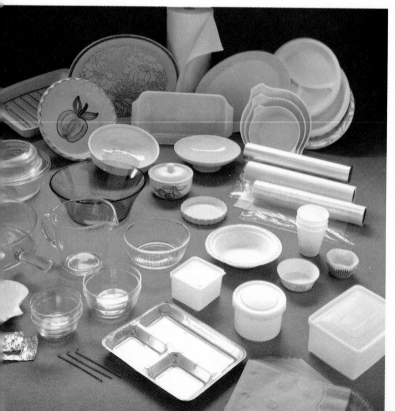

Microwave No

Facts About Utensils

Heat-Resistant Glass	**Measuring cups, baby bottles, oven casseroles, loaf dishes, platters, utility dishes, cake dishes**

This material is fine for microwave cooking because microwaves pass through the dish without heating the dish itself. There's a wide variety of shapes and sizes. Fire King, Pyrex and Creative Glass are some of the well-known brands. Glass-ceramic is particularly durable and good for use with the Browner. Look for labels such as "Oven Proof" or "Good for Microwave." *Avoid using anything with a metal part, such as a screw or clamp, or metal trim.*

Glass, Unglazed Ceramic	**Casseroles, utility dishes, pie plates, cake dishes, dinnerware**

Corning Ware and Corelle, except the closed-handle cup, are some of the well-known brands that can be used. *Cook-Serve covers and Centura dinnerware—a glazed glass-ceramic—are NOT suitable.*

China and Pottery	**Dinnerware, porcelain soufflé dishes and ring molds, pottery casseroles and stoneware Bundt dishes**

Brands that don't have metal trim or metallic glaze or metal in their composition are suitable. Generally these are used for warm-ups. But sometimes it's convenient to cook in serving dishes of this type. They absorb some heat from the food while it's cooking. Test as described on page 8.

Plastics	**Dinnerware, plastic wrap, oven-roasting bags, cooking pouches, mini-cake maker, styrofoam**

Dinnerware should be used only for reheating and NEVER with the Browner or Stay Hot. *Melamine Ware is not suitable, even for reheating.* If you have another brand, test one dish before heating food. Place 1/4 cup of water in the dish and heat on High to boiling. If there's warping at the water line, or odor, the dish is not suitable.

Dishwasher-safe, plastic storage containers are suitable for reheating food with a low fat or low sugar content. Too much fat or sugar content, as in a gravy or dessert sauce, blisters or distorts the plastic because of the higher temperatures reached.

Plastic wrap is ideal for covering utensils not having their own lids. It's also good for wrapping around some foods. Remember to pierce the wrap to allow steam to escape. After standing time, steam is still hot enough to burn, so remove the wrap carefully. Do not use plastic wrap with the Browner or Stay Hot. It will melt.

Use oven bags without the metal twist. Tie them with string, rubber band or a self-knot. Pierce the bag several places to allow steam to escape. Use caution when you open oven bags and cooking pouches.

Facts About Utensils

Paper, plastic-coated or non-coated

Dinnerware, wax paper, paper towels and napkins, cupcake papers, cups and bowls

Paper products are suitable except when using the Browner or Stay Hot. For storage, staple or tape on a second paper plate as a cover. Mark the contents and heating time on the rim of the plate. Be sure to *remove staples* before reheating.

Nylon reinforcements in Teri brand towels melt when they contact grease.

DO NOT POP CORN or use newspapers to absorb bacon grease.

Straw and wood

Baskets, bowls, plank board

Do not use these with the Browner or Stay Hot. Use them for very short warm-ups. Microwaves will dry out the utensil and cause cracking. Reheating bread on a bread board is handy and won't damage the wood. Long cooking will dry out the wood and cause it to crack.

Sometimes it's convenient to leave a wooden spoon in sauce or pudding for easy stirring. The spoon gets warm but is still suitable for brief cooking times.

Lacquer Ware

Trays, bowls

These are not suitable because they may crack or discolor.

Shells

Scalloped baking shells

Use these for short warm-ups or short cooking.

Metal, if allowed by microwave-oven instructions

Aluminum foil, 7/8-inch-deep convenience trays, skewers and microwave-oven meat rack are allowed in Thermatronic and some other brands.

Allow 1-inch clearance from stainless-steel oven walls for all usable metals. Always be sure a larger amount of food is used than the amount of metal.

Use foil for shielding small ends of meats and poultry. Apply it sparingly and as smoothly as possible. Crinkled foil can cause *arcing* or *sparkling*. Foil can be used to cover food during standing time and can be used with the Stay Hot.

Metal twist-ties cannot be used on oven bags because the metal gets hot and may set the paper covering on fire.

Warming & Heating

One of the major uses cooks find for microwave ovens is reheating previously cooked foods. Leftovers or planned-overs taste freshly cooked. Because foods can be heated so quickly, there is no loss of flavor or drying out. In fact, many foods, such as pancakes, vegetables and rare pieces of meat which are difficult to reheat conventionally, are successfully reheated in the microwave oven. Many people double the recipe they're cooking and plan to reheat the second part a day or two later. Or make your own convenience foods by freezing the extras. You'll find yourself using planned-overs as you become more familiar with your microwave oven.

Besides reheating, you'll discover lots of foods that need only to be heated and served, such as rolls, doughnuts, pies, cookies, hor d'ouevres and even baby food heated right in the jar or bottle. Never heat anything in a tightly sealed container—steam may cause it to explode. Always remove jar-tops. Perforate plastic covers and bags.

If someone is going to be late for a meal, serve his plate along with everyone else's, cover with plastic wrap and refrigerate. Later you simply put it in the oven and in a very few minutes it's piping hot and tastes freshly cooked.

SINGLE-SERVING WARM-UPS

FOOD	DIRECTIONS
1 mug coffee, instant or reheat	Heat on High for 1-1/2 to 2-1/4 minutes
1 mug hot cocoa	Heat on High for 2-1/4 minutes. Add marshmallow the last 30 seconds.
1 cup soup, instant or reheat	Heat on High for 1-1/2 to 2-1/4 minutes
1 roll: donut, dinner roll, sweet roll, muffin or bagel	Put on paper napkin. Heat on Low for 3/4 to 1 minute.
1 bowl cereal, instant	Add water to bowl. Cook on High for 2 minutes.
1 tortilla	Spread with butter and fold over. Heat on High for 3/4 minute.
1 (10-oz.) burrito	Put on paper plate or towel. Heat on High for 2 minutes.
2 tamales	Heat on High for 4 to 5 minutes in covered dish.
1 (4-oz.) pizza wedge, cooked	Put on paper towel. Heat on Low for 1-3/4 minutes.
2 small round pizzas, frozen	Use upper shelf. Put pizzas on metal rack in utility dish. Heat on Medium for 3 minutes. Brown.
1 pastrami sandwich (5-oz.), frozen	Heat on Low for 1 to 2 minutes.
1 hot dog and bun	Wrap in paper napkin. Heat on High for 1/2 minute.
1 (1/3-lb.) ground-meat patty	Use upper shelf. Cook on High for 2 to 2-1/2 minutes. Brown.
1 chicken thigh, frozen	Heat on Medium for 2-1/2 minutes.
1 chicken leg and thigh, frozen	Heat on Medium for 3-1/2 minutes.
6 fish sticks, breaded, frozen	Heat on Medium for 3 minutes. Put on metal rack in utility dish. Crisp on Stay Hot.
1 dinner plate of food, cooked	Reheat on High for 1-1/4 to 1-1/2 minutes.
1 medium-size apple, uncooked	Core. Cook on High for 2 minutes. Let stand 3 minutes. Heat on High for 3/4 minute.
1 piece of pie. 2-crust	Heat on High for 3/4 minute.
1 (4-oz.) baby bottle with milk	Heat on High for 40 to 50 seconds. Shake well and test temperature on your wrist.
1 jar of baby food	Remove lid. Warm 15 to 20 seconds on High. Test temperature before serving.

Five-Day Cooking School

This Cooking School will teach you the basic techniques of microwave cooking, so you can cook a full-course meal without checking the instruction book constantly. Nor will you have a kitchen catastrophe because you pushed the wrong button, used an inappropriate utensil, or misjudged cooking time.

Follow these Cooking School instructions. Practice different methods such as defrosting, softening, warming-up, baking, browning, heating and all the other techniques used by experts. This Cooking School gives you step-by-step procedures for everything you need to know.

Here are menus for 5 days with tips and procedures to make you as efficient as your microwave, and even shopping lists so you'll know what to buy.

You don't have to use a day's menus all in the same day, unless you want to. Take a meal at a time. Spread these meals out over a period that is convenient for you. With each meal you complete, no matter how simple, you'll be that much closer to becoming an experienced microwave cook.

First Day

BREAKFAST
Frozen Orange Juice
Sweet Roll
Instant Coffee, page 11

Soften frozen orange juice in the can. Remove one end of juice can before placing in oven on High for 15 to 30 seconds. Let stand 5 minutes before adding water. Heat water for coffee or previously perked coffee in your own mug. Set roll on a paper plate or towel. Heat on Low for 1/2 to 1 minute. Heat a bakery item only warm to the touch because it will be hotter in the center.

LUNCH
Bacon-Tomato Sandwich
Baked Apples, page 168
Milk

Soften package of bacon on High for 15 seconds. Let stand for 5 minutes and slices will separate easily. Cover with paper towel to prevent grease spatters in the oven. Cook bacon on a metal meat rack or on pleated paper towels. Cook Baked Apples right in the serving dish.

DINNER
Chicken Parmesan, page 63
Corn-on-Cob, page 120
Instant Potatoes, page 132

Cook fresh corn-on-the-cob after cooking chicken and let stand at the table.

Second Day

BREAKFAST
Juice
Caramel Biscuit Ring, page 147
Instant Cocoa, page 11

Brown the Caramel Biscuit Ring to help caramelize the sauce. Use your own mug or cup for cocoa. Don't forget the marshmallow!

LUNCH
Cup of Soup, page 11
Hot Dog and Bun, page 11
Fresh Fruit

Heat instant soup, canned soup or leftover soup in a soup bowl or mug. Heat the hot dog and bun after it's all together—mustard, relish and catsup, too—wrapped in a paper napkin. If the bun seems too soft, re-heat it separately.

DINNER
Stag Chili, page 100
Cauliflower, page 120
Warmed French Bread, page 152
Pie and Ice Cream

If the ground beef for Stag Chili is frozen, see the Defrosting Uncooked Meats Table, page 73. Covered Chili will keep warm on Stay Hot while the uncovered French bread is crisping right beside it.

Third Day

BREAKFAST
Frozen Fruit
Bill's Bran Muffins, page 148
Cereal, page 151
Hot Tea

Pierce package of frozen fruit and soften on High for 15 seconds. Let stand a few minutes. Cook muffins as they are requested. This batter keeps up to 6 weeks in the refrigerator. Cook hot cereal in the serving bowl.

LUNCH
Hamburger Sandwich
JELL-O®
Milk

Measure water for JELL-O® and heat in a glass measuring cup. Choose a size large enough to accommodate all of the cold JELL-O® ingredients. Refrigerate in the measuring cup. Cook the hamburger patty between two paper plates. Remove the top plate before browning.

DINNER
Pork Chops, page 77
Baked Potatoes, page 122
Frozen Broccoli, page 119

Bake the potatoes first and set aside in a terry towel or wrap in foil. Then cook the pork chops, brown on the top side and serve.

Fourth Day

BREAKFAST
Scrambled Eggs, page 143
Bagel with Cream Cheese,
    page 11
Fresh Fruit

Open foil and soften cream cheese on High for 15 seconds. Let stand for 5 minutes. Eggs are a delicate food to cook. Watch cooking closely to avoid toughening. Heat the bagel on a paper plate or paper towel after eggs are cooked.

LUNCH
Ham and Cheese Sandwich
Sliced Tomatoes and
    Carrot Sticks
Cottage Cheese and Peaches

Make the sandwich after breakfast. Wrap it in wax paper and refrigerate. At lunchtime, loosen the wrapping and warm on High for 15 seconds. Ham and cheese flavors blend better when the chill is removed. Fix fresh vegetables during standing time of sandwich.

DINNER
Barbecued Halibut Steaks,
    page 88
Rice, page 150
Frozen Spinach, page 122
Cookies

Prepare the rice first and let it stand while the fish is cooking.

Fifth Day

BREAKFAST
Fruit Juice
Poached Egg, page 143
Sausage, page 77
Toast

Cook sausage on the metal meat rack in utility dish or on pleated paper towels on a paper plate. Poach the egg while the bread is in the toaster. Check to be sure the toaster and microwave oven are not operating on the same circuit.

LUNCH
Reuben Sandwich, page 39
Tossed Green Salad
Crackers

If crackers need freshening and crisping, place on a paper plate or paper towel. Heat on High for 15 seconds.

DINNER
Roast Beef, page 75
Instant Scalloped Potatoes,
    page 130
Marie's Tomato Stack-Ups,
    page 110
Old-Fashioned Carrot Cake
    with Cream-Cheese Frosting,
    pages 158 and 159

Bake the cake before preparing the roast. Frost and serve the cake right in the dish. Cook vegetable for Marie's Tomato Stack-Ups. Assemble them before roasting the meat. Heat through during the meat's standing time. Study the Beef and Veal Cooking Techniques on page 40 and 41 and the meat cooking tables, beginning on page 74 before starting the roast. Insert a meat thermometer after cooking to determine doneness, or use the Temp-Matic™ temperature probe if your oven has this feature.

Five-Day Cooking School Shopping List

Check what you already have on hand. Buy the correct quantities for your family.

FIRST THREE DAYS

Meat
bacon
1 cut-up chicken
hot dogs
1 lb. ground beef, lean
hamburger patties
pork chops

Baking Supplies
brown sugar
cinnamon
chopped nuts
raisin bran

Frozen Foods
orange juice
mixed fruit
chopped broccoli or spinach

Fresh Vegetables
tomatoes
baking apples
corn-on-the-cob
cauliflower
green peppers

Canned & Packaged Items
soup
2 (16-oz.) cans kidney beans
1 (16-oz.) can tomatoes
1 pkg. chili seasoning
salad oil
JELL-O®
instant onion
1 (8-oz.) can tomato sauce
instant coffee
instant cocoa
instant potatoes

Dairy
Parmesan cheese
butter
buttermilk
eggs

Paper Supplies
paper towels
paper plates
cupcake papers

Bread
sweet roll
sandwich bread
1 (8-oz.) pkg. refrigerator biscuits
hot dog buns
French bread
hamburger buns

NEXT TWO DAYS

Meat
ham slices
fish fillets
1 (3-lb.) beef roast
corned beef slices
sausage, links or bulk

Baking Supplies
cookies
powdered sugar
granulated sugar
flour
salad oil
chopped walnuts
raisins

Frozen Foods
chopped spinach or broccoli

Fresh Vegetables
tomatoes
carrots
radishes
lettuce
cabbage
onion

Canned & Packaged Items
peach halves
salad dressing
sauerkraut
Thousand Island dressing
rice
instant scalloped potatoes

Dairy
eggs
1 (8-oz.) pkg. cream cheese
milk
cheese slices
margarine
cottage cheese
American cheese
Swiss cheese, grated
whipped cream

Bread
bagels
sandwich bread
rye bread

Your Microwave-Menu Planner

Now you're anxious to try your new skills. You have learned the basic techniques in the Five-Day Cooking School and you are ready! To help you get started, here are some menus with page-number references for the recipes.

If you want to use one of your favorite conventional recipes instead of one listed in these menus, just turn to pages 17 and 18 for conversion instructions.

When cooking several items for one meal, you will quickly learn to take advantage of stored heat. Some items will remain warm enough to serve without further heating. Some will require reheating just before serving, which can be done quickly, sometimes right in the serving dish. Notice the recommended *standing times* for some items and plan your cooking schedule accordingly. Remember your Thermatronic has a Stay-Hot control to use for keeping food warm during standing time.

Before you begin, plan and organize your cooking time so you take full advantage of the speed of microwave cookery. Check each recipe to see how much time is needed for thawing, cooking and standing. Use these times to work on other recipes. Decide on a cooking plan so everything is ready to serve at the same time. If you can't keep all the information in your head, write it down. Make yourself a schedule for the first few meals you plan and check off each step as you do it. You'll soon get used to the method and the shorter cooking times, and you'll be doing it automatically.

Oriental Ham Kabobs, page 61
Microwave Rice, page 150
Fresh Vegetable Platter, page 117

French Stuffed Hamburgers, page 45
Scalloped Potatoes, page 112
Autumn Apple Pie, page 163

Corn Pudding, page 142
Fruit Salad
Hot French Herb Bread, page 148
Cheese

Roast Beef, page 75
Mashed Potatoes
Gravy, page 129
Spinach-Cheese Bake, page 110
Cherry Cobbler, page 167

Clam-Potato Chowder, page 38
Sally Lunn Dill Bread, page 146
Sherbet

Beef Enchiladas with Cheese, page 105
Broccoli, page 119
JELL-O®

Meat Loaf, page 48
Baked Potatoes, page 122
Glazed Carrots, page 114
Chili-Cheese Corn Bread, page 146

Roast Chicken, page 79
Creamed Peas and Onions
Rice with Vegetables, page 118
Elegant Bread Pudding, page 162

Rack of Lamb, page 79
Microwave Rice, page 150
Cauliflower, page 120
Cheese Sauce, page 124
Cappuccino, page 30

Converting Recipes is Easy

You will undoubtedly want to cook some of your favorite conventional recipes in your microwave oven. With a little thought and experimenting, you can convert nearly any recipe. Write down the microwave version and then you have two ways to prepare family favorites.

LOOK FOR A SIMILAR RECIPE IN A MICROWAVE COOKBOOK

In this or another microwave cookbook, you can probably find a recipe very similar to your favorite. Look for one with the same amount and type of main ingredient, and in the *same form,* such as ground meat, frozen or defrosted ingredients, fresh, canned, or whatever the form may be.

Then compare the other ingredients, such as vegetables or pasta. Notice how the microwave recipe deals with the other ingredients. The microwave recipe will probably call for less total liquid than a conventional recipe. This is normal for many foods. Follow the microwave-recipe recommendation.

The type and amount of spices is not important in converting recipes. You can use the spices called for in the conventional recipe so you get the same flavor. Some microwave cooks use less spice because the flavor doesn't seem to cook away as much in a microwave oven.

Follow the procedure for the microwave recipe, using the ingredients and spices from the conventional recipe. Cooking time may require adjustment; see page 19.

IF YOU DON'T FIND A SIMILAR RECIPE

Find recipes in the same general category, such as meat casseroles, vegetable casseroles, pies or bar cookies. Notice how the ingredients are grouped together and the cooking time. Study several recipes and write down a procedure you think will work with the ingredients of the recipe you are converting. Make the adjustments listed below, including cooking time, and then try the procedure. You will then probably make some small changes for an even-better result.

In addition to checking specific recipes, be sure to read the introductory pages in this book. You'll find tables listing cooking times and lots of information to help you.

If the Recipe is Oven-Prepared—To convert a recipe designed for a conventional oven so you can prepare it in your microwave, reduce the amount of liquid to 3/4 and reduce cooking time to 1/4. For example, if a recipe calls for 1 cup liquid, reduce it to 3/4 cup. The type of liquid doesn't matter. A casserole that cooks in 1 hour in a conventional oven will cook in about 15 minutes in a microwave. Microwave cooking is so fast that properly heated foods don't have a chance to dry out.

If the Recipe is Prepared on a Stove Top—When cooked in a microwave, these recipes usually take more than 1/4 of the usual time. Items with a lot of water, such as rice or noodles, cook in about the same length of time as on a stove top. Using recipes in this book as a guide, cook slightly less than the recommended time, check, then cook more as needed. Add another 15 to 30 seconds, then check again.

Don't expect to dry-out or cook-down foods that have a lot of liquid, such as spaghetti sauce. These will cook-down on a stove top because they cook a long time and steam escapes. In a microwave, these foods are done before there is much evaporation, so the amount of liquid used must be reduced.

When To Add Salt—Salt tends to draw out moisture. If you don't want a lot of liquid, add salt after cooking. Some French recipes require liquids to make an elegant sauce which is then poured over the food. In these cases, add the salt before cooking.

HOW TO CONVERT RECIPES IN THIS COOKBOOK FOR YOUR BRAND OF MICROWAVE OVEN

At this time, there is no standardization of microwave-power levels among various brands. Power settings range from a single power level, to 2 or 3 power levels on some brands, to 10 settings on others. If you own a brand other than Thermador, here is a simple way to convert the power settings mentioned in this book to use with your oven. This same method can be used to convert recipes in any microwave-oven cookbook to use the power settings on your particular oven.

You can determine the power levels of your own oven by the amount of time it takes to bring 1 cup of lukewarm water to a boil. The time is measured from the start until bubbles just begin to rise.

To find the power level of your oven on High:
1. Measure 1 cup of lukewarm water (neither hot nor cold to the touch) in a 1-cup glass measure.
2. Put the cup of water into your microwave oven and press the High setting.
3. Set the timer for 10 minutes. Observe and record the time when the bubbles just begin to rise. This will happen before the end of the timed period.
4. Notice the amount of time it took for bubbles to rise and find that number in the table below.
5. Write in the power setting on your oven that corresponds with the Thermador power setting.

Time for Water Test	Thermador Power Setting	Equivalent Power Setting On My Oven
2 to 3 min.	High	_____
3-1/2 to 4-1/2 min.	Medium	_____
4-1/2 to 5-1/2 min.	Low	_____

Repeat the test with another cup of lukewarm water, using the next lower power setting. Continue until you have the settings on your oven that correspond to High, Medium and Low for the recipes in this cookbook. Now, when a recipe calls for High, Medium or Low, you'll know which power setting you can use to cook it in your particular microwave oven.

If your oven boils water in a time longer than 3 minutes but less than 3-1/2 minutes, that means this setting on your particular oven falls between our Medium and High setting. If the recipe calls for High, add cooking time. If it calls for Medium, use less cooking time.

After you have found the power setting on your oven that corresponds to our Low setting, you may have still more settings on your oven. Refer to the literature that came with your oven for recipes using these settings.

If you do not have any power setting that is near our Low setting, don't use recipes calling for Low in your oven. Most recipes intended to be cooked on Low cannot successfully be cooked at a higher power level.

THINGS THAT AFFECT COOKING TIME

Several things affect cooking time. It's always best to undercook, check the food, and then cook a little longer.

Starting Temperature—Chilled foods, fresh from the refrigerator or barely thawed, take more time than foods at room temperature.

Density of the Main Ingredient—Dense foods take longer. Examples: A potato bakes in about 4 minutes on High. An apple of similar size bakes in only 1-1/2 minutes or a little longer on High. The potato is more dense and it takes the microwaves longer to penetrate and cook through.

Form of Main Ingredient—A single mass of food takes longer than the same amount in smaller pieces. A meat loaf cooks as a single mass and takes longer than the same amount of meat which has been cubed or sliced. Plain ground beef, cooked without added ingredients, cooks faster than sliced or cubed meat.

Amount of Food—More food takes longer to cook. As a rule, if you double the amount of food, add slightly less than 50% more cooking time.

Size and Shape of Container—If the container is too deep, it takes longer to cook the center and the edges may be overdone. If the container is too shallow, the food cooks faster but the edges will be overdone.

Amount of Liquid—All liquids heat in the same length of time. One cup of liquid reaches boiling in 2 to 2-1/2 minutes on High. A smaller amount of liquid reaches boiling temperature in less time. For low-moisture foods, 6 minutes a pound on High is a good estimate of cooking time. For high-moisture foods, such as spaghetti sauce, estimate cooking time by referring to recipes in this book.

MEASURING TEMPERATURE

Some foods, such as meats, can be cooked using temperature as a guide to doneness. There are several ways to do it.

Conventional meat thermometers or oven thermometers are designed for use in a conventional oven and **must not be used in a microwave oven during cooking.** You can use a conventional thermometer by removing the food, inserting the thermometer and reading the temperature reached. If it is not high enough, remove the conventional thermometer and return the food to the oven. Test again later. Refer to temperature-testing tables for meats, pages 41 and 42, for suggested internal temperatures.

Microwave meat thermometers are designed to be used inside a microwave oven, during cooking. You just insert the microwave thermometer so it doesn't touch bone or the cooking dish and leave it in place during cooking. To check temperature, open the door and take the reading.

Temperature probes, such as the Thermador Temp-Matic, are connected to the microwave oven and are used during cooking. Insert the probe in the food to be cooked, set the oven control for the desired temperature, and the oven will turn off automatically when that temperature is reached.

Pop-up indicators are sometimes included with turkeys and are already in place when purchased. In a conventional oven, these are calibrated to indicate doneness. These may be used in your microwave oven but will not pop up at the end of microwave cooking. The suggested internal temperature for poultry is 150°F to 160°F (66°C to 71°C) when removed from the microwave oven; finished temperature is 170°F (77°C) after standing. The indicator should pop up during standing time when temperature is reached. The poultry is then ready to carve and serve. As indicated in the Poultry Roasting Table, pages 79 and 80, some poultry is wrapped in foil during standing time to help hold heat in the meat.

How To Use A Temperature Probe

These instructions specifically apply to the Temp-Matic™ probe available with certain models of Thermador microwave ovens. Other brands of microwave ovens use temperature probes on some models. The cooking tables and information given here are generally applicable to any brand, however you should check the instruction booklet for your microwave to be sure you observe any special procedures or precautions.

HOW IT WORKS

A reliable indication of doneness is the temperature reached by food as it cooks. A temperature-sensing probe is inserted into the food being cooked to measure temperature directly. You set the oven controls for the desired *temperature*, rather than the length of time to cook. When the food reaches the desired temperature, the oven shuts off automatically. Use the temperature tables in this section and on pages 41 and 42 to cook foods to a desired temperature.

Recipes and cooking tables elsewhere in this book give recommended cooking *times* and microwave-power settings. These times are approximate and will vary depending on initial temperature of the food, size, shape and other factors, such as the amount of bone, fat or sugar in the food.

GENERAL INSTRUCTIONS FOR USING TEMP-MATIC TEMPERATURE PROBE

The Temp-Matic temperature probe is especially designed for microwave cooking. DO NOT use it in a conventional oven.

Insert the probe so that at least 1 inch of the probe (the sensor) is in the food. Best results are achieved if probe is inserted into the center-most part of the food on a slant, avoiding fat, bone and gristle. Do not allow the probe to touch the bottom or sides of the cooking dish. For liquids, the handle on the Temp-Matic probe can be placed over the edge of the dish. This supports the probe so it does not touch the bottom or sides of the dish.

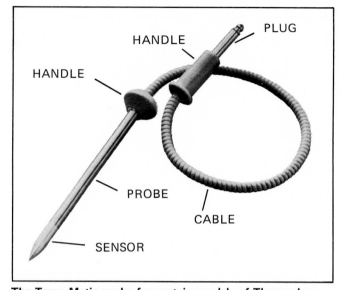

The Temp-Matic probe for certain models of Thermador Microwave Ovens measures temperature of the food as it cooks; oven shuts off automatically when desired food temperature is reached. Some other brands offer a similar temperature-probe feature.

Select microwave-power level—Low, Medium or High—desired for cooking. When the cooking tables in this section give you a choice of power settings, the lower setting will take longer but require less attention.

Push the Temp-Matic plug completely into the receptacle in the oven wall. Be sure the cable does not touch the oven walls, the stirrer or the Browner element in the top of the oven. If the Browner or Stay Hot is used after cooking, be absolutely certain the cable does not touch the element. Close the oven door.

Set the desired temperature on the Temp-Matic dial. This eliminates setting minutes on the timer.

Press the Start button on the control panel.

When the desired internal temperature is reached, the oven turns off automatically and a buzzer sounds. Opening the oven door stops the buzzer. Remove the Temp-Matic probe from the oven, using the handle at the plug end. Do not pull on the cable.

If the buzzer sounds sooner than your estimated cooking time based on the accompanying tables, the probe may not have been inserted properly, or it may have slipped out of place. In either case, reposition the probe and continue cooking. Be sure the probe can be used effectively for the type of food you are cooking—see the accompanying tables.

To determine actual temperature of the food as it cooks, turn the Temp-Matic dial slowly to a lower temperature setting until buzzer sounds,

then reset to the desired temperature and press the Start button to turn oven on again.

The Temp-Matic cable and handles may become too hot to handle during cooking. If necessary, use pot holders to prevent burns when removing probe from food.

Do not leave the Temp-Matic temperature probe in the Thermatronic oven when it is not being used in the preparation of food.

RECOMMENDED TEMPERATURE SETTINGS
FOR USE WITH TEMPERATURE PROBE

Food	Recommended Microwave-Power Setting	Temp-Matic™ Setting		Procedure
Beverages	High	Warm to drink – 120°F to 130°F (49°C to 54°F) Steaming – 170°F (77°C)		Use a glass measuring-cup or a pitcher when heating more than 1 cup.
Casserole	Medium or High	Mixed – 150°F (66°C) Layered – 160°F (71°C)		Do not use Temp-Matic for cooking casseroles containing raw meat. Use to check temperature when reheating. If possible stir mixed casserole before standing time. Cover, let stand at least 5 minutes before serving.
Dips	Low or Medium	120°F to 140°F (49°C to 60°C) depending on ingredients		Mix ingredients thoroughly before heating. Stir before serving.
Meat	See Separate Tables on pages 24, 41, 42			
Meat loaf	Low or Medium	Beef or Lamb	145°F to 160°F (63°C to 71°C)	Beef, lamb, pork or a combination may be used. For best results use no more than 1 cup of liquid for 1-1/2 pounds of meat. Let stand covered or place uncovered under Browner for 10 minutes before serving.
		Pork or Combination	160°F to 170°F (71°C to 77°C)	
Reheat Planned-overs	Medium or High	150°F to 160°F (66°C to 71°C)		Cover for faster heating. Stir before serving.
Soup	High	Broth – 150°F (66°C) Chunky – 160°F (71°C)		Place probe in center of liquid. Stir before serving.

Where there is a choice of microwave power settings, the lower setting will usually require less attention, but will take longer to heat.

How To Use A Temperature Probe

Using the Temp-Matic probe gives just the degree of doneness you prefer—automatically.

The oven should not be operated empty with or without the Temp-Matic plug in the receptacle.

Cover foods whenever possible during cooking to shorten cooking time. Do not cover foods that you want to develop a dry surface.

Do not allow the probe to touch metal foil used to shield parts of food because it will cause arcing.

After use, wash probe in warm, soapy water; rinse and dry. Do not immerse in water or wash in a dishwasher.

Always use glass or glass-ceramic dishes when cooking with the Temp-Matic temperature probe. Meat may be placed on the specially designed metal meat rack—available from Thermador—as long as the Temp-Matic probe does not touch the metal.

ROASTING MEATS WITH A TEMPERATURE PROBE

Most tender cuts of beef, veal, lamb and pork can be roasted successfully using your choice of power setting. However, Low power generally produces the best, most-tender results with the least attention, rotating and checking. This is particularly true for less-tender cuts such as sirloin tips and rump roasts. A long, thin roast will take less time to cook than a short, thick roast of the same weight. Symmetrically shaped roasts will cook more uniformly than irregularly shaped roasts. For uniform cooking, meat is turned and the cooking dish rotated one-half turn when the probe is placed in the food or at the halfway point in cooking.

GENERAL INSTRUCTIONS FOR ROASTING MEAT

Place meat fat side down on special meat rack (available from Thermador), or you can use a glass trivet in the bottom of the baking dish.

Estimate total cooking time, based on maximum minutes per pound in the meat-roasting table on page 24.

Cook with microwave for one half the estimated total cooking time at recommended power setting from chart. Use microwave timer to signal when one half of total time has elasped.

For example: a four-pound boneless rump roast cooked to rare (120°F before standing time) will take approximately 12 to 14 minutes per pound on Low, according to the table on page 24. Calculate the maximum approximate total cooking time by multiplying the weight of the roast—4 pounds—by the maximum time given on the table for rare—14 minutes per pound: 4 x 14 = 56 minutes. Divide the total cooking time (56 minutes) in half to determine the length of time to set the timer to cook the roast on the first side: 56 ÷ 2 = 28 minutes.

How To Use A Temperature Probe

When timer signals, turn meat fat side up and rotate dish one half turn. Insert Temp-Matic probe at least 1 inch into center of meat. Be sure probe does not touch metal rack or cooking dish. Avoid fat, bone and gristle. Push the plug end into the receptacle in the oven wall. Close the door.

Set desired temperature on Temp-Matic dial. Push Start button. Continue to cook until buzzer sounds, indicating that meat has reached the desired internal temperature.

Allow meat to stand the length of time indicated on the table, to finish cooking and set the juices for easier carving. Internal temperature will rise about 15°F to 20°F (8°C to 11°C) during standing time. Meat may stand in the Thermatronic oven with the Stay Hot turned on or it may stand elsewhere covered with foil.

SPECIAL TIPS

Cooking time will vary depending on starting temperature of meat. Testing for this table was done with meat starting at average refrigerator temperature. Very cold meat will take longer to cook. Room-temperature or warm meat will take far less time to cook. Meat defrosted by microwave power, even after standing, is sometimes still quite cold in the center, yet room temperature or warm on the exterior. Best results will be obtained if the temperature of the roast is as equal throughout as possible, otherwise the outside of the roast may be overdone.

The bone and fat content of a roast will have a definite effect on the way it cooks. A rib or standing roast may require a longer cooking time than a boneless roast of the same cut. Occasionally the interior meat directly adjacent to the bone will remain pink even though the Temp-Matic meat thermometer registers a finished temperature. A large amount of fat within a roast can affect cooking and cause inaccurate readings on a meat thermometer or temperature probe.

If the buzzer sounds too soon—ahead of approximate total cooking time—double-check probe placement to be sure it is in the center of the meat and in a muscle. When cooking a small thin roast, for example a sirloin, if the Temp-Matic is set for a low temperature, it may signal immediately after being inserted into the meat and plugged into the oven. Remove the probe; insert it again carefully in the centermost section of the roast. If Temp-Matic still signals, reset the temperature about 5°F (3°C) higher.

Large areas of fat can cause overcooking. When the meat is turned over, cover with foil any areas beginning to overcook. Occasionally ham or other cured meats may overcook in some areas due to the high concentration of salt used in the curing process. Cover any fast-cooking areas with foil. *BE CERTAIN FOIL DOES NOT TOUCH TEMP-MATIC PROBE AS IT WILL CAUSE ARCING.*

Cover ham with wax paper during cooking. Shield small end of ham with foil during first half of cooking time. Remove foil, turn ham over and rotate dish one-half turn; insert Temp-Matic probe. A very cold, thick ham may require longer to cook than indicated on the table.

FOODS NOT RECOMMENDED FOR THE TEMP-MATIC TEMPERATURE PROBE

Frozen Foods—Probe should not be forced into frozen foods. However, after defrosting, probe can be inserted, if appropriate.

Starchy Vegetables (such as potatoes or yams)—These foods have a tendency to stick to the probe.

Candy Making or Simmering (such as stews or pot-roasts)—When food must come to a boil and/or simmer for a long time, the temperature probe reaches temperature before the food is done.

Individual Food Items Cooked at the Same Time—Variation in size, shape or moisture content can affect cooking time. Therefore, the Temp-Matic probe in one food item of a batch may not correctly indicate the temperature of the other items.

Whole Poultry—Not recommended for probe cooking because it is very difficult to position the probe correctly to accurately determine the degree of doneness, due to the large proportion of bone to meat and the general composition of the bird. Refer to the roasting table on pages 79 and 80 for suggested minutes-per-pound and the power setting. However, good results can be achieved cooking a turkey breast using the Temp-Matic. See table on page 24.

TV-Dinner-Type Foil Trays—For safe and accurate use of the Temp-Matic probe, avoid using it with foil trays because the probe could contact the metal tray and cause arcing.

Micro-Mate Browning Dishes—The Temp-Matic temperature probe should not be used with browning dishes. The accuracy of the sensor may be affected if it should come in contact with the bottom of the dish.

How To Use A Temperature Probe

RECOMMENDED TEMPERATURE SETTINGS
FOR ROASTING MEAT WITH TEMPERATURE PROBE

Type of Roast	Recommended Power Setting	Approximate Cooking Time – Minutes per pound		Temp-Matic Set °F	Temp-Matic Set °C	Standing Time
Beef (Bone-in) Standing Rib (Large End)	Low	Very rare	9-11	110	43	5 to 10 min.
		Rare	11-13	120	49	5 to 10 min.
		Medium	13-15	130	54	10 min.
		Well done	15-16	140	60	15 min.
Standing Rib (Small End)	Low	Very rare	8- 9	110	43	5 min.
		Rare	9-11	120	49	5 to 10 min.
		Medium	11-13	130	54	10 min.
		Well done	13-15	140	60	15 min.
Beef (Boneless) Rolled Rib (Large End) Rolled Rump (high quality)	Low	Very rare	10-12	110	43	5 to 10 min.
		Rare	12-14	120	49	5 to 10 min.
		Medium	14-15	130	54	10 min.
		Well done	15-16	140	60	15 min.
Tenderloin Rolled Rib (Small End) Top Loin Sirloin Tip (high quality)	Low	Very rare	8- 9	110	43	5 to 10 min.
		Rare	9-10	120	49	5 to 10 min.
		Medium	10-12	130	54	10 min.
		Well done	12-14	140	60	15 min.
Pork—Fresh Loin (bone-in)	Low	Med. well	12-15	160	71	15 min.
Loin (boneless)		Med. well	10-14	160	71	15 min.
Pork – Smoked Ham (fully cooked) Canned	Medium		10-13	115	46	10 min.
Lamb Leg (bone-in)	Low	Medium	13-15	140	60	10 to 15 min.
		Well done	15-16	160	71	15 min.
Leg or Shoulder (boneless)	Low	Medium	11-13	140	60	10 to 15 min.
		Well done	13-15	160	71	15 min.
Poultry Turkey Breast or half (insert probe in thickest area of breast)	Medium	Well	14-16	155	68	15 min.

Recommended internal temperature settings may vary from conventional roasting charts because microwave-cooked meats do more cooking after the microwaves have stopped and the internal temperature rises more during standing time.

Appetizers & Beverages

Microwave cookery makes entertaining easy. Prepare delicious hot Mexican Chocolate while your guests are hanging up their coats. Or serve a spicy toddy—try Hot Wine Cranberry Punch.

Appetizers can be readied the night before. When you hear the doorbell, pop them into your microwave oven. They'll be hot and tasty in no-time. With a microwave, you can plan ahead so your party food is ready to cook when you come home from a busy day.

Appetizer Meatballs

Prepare ahead for a quick treat.

1 egg, slightly beaten
1/3 cup milk
1/3 cup fine, dry bread crumbs
1 tablespoon instant minced onion

1 teaspoon salt
1 teaspoon sugar
1/4 teaspoon allspice
1 lb. lean ground meat

Combine ingredients and form into 1-inch balls. Place on wire rack in 7-1/2" x 12" utility dish. Raise shelf. Cook on High for 4 to 6 minutes. Brown 3 to 5 minutes. Makes about 25 meatballs.

Cheese Puffs

Cheese flavor—with a difference.

3 green onions, finely chopped
1 cup grated cheddar cheese

1/2 cup mayonnaise
24 toast rounds

Combine green onions with cheese and mayonnaise. Spread on toast rounds. In 8-1/4-inch shallow baking dish heat half the rounds on Medium for 1-1/2 to 2-1/2 minutes or until bubbly. Turn baking dish once during cooking. Repeat with remaining puffs. Serve hot. Makes 24 appetizers.

Stuffed Mushrooms

Make plenty of these—they'll go fast!

4 slices bacon, diced
1/4 cup minced onion
2 tablespoons minced green pepper
1/2 teaspoon salt
1/2 teaspoon Worcestershire sauce

1 (3-oz.) pkg. cream cheese
1 lb. small fresh mushrooms
1/2 cup soft bread crumbs
1 tablespoon butter or margarine

Combine bacon, onion, and green pepper in 4-cup measure. Cover with paper towel. Cook on High for 4 minutes, stirring once. Pour off fat. Mix in salt, Worcestershire sauce and cream cheese. Wash and dry mushrooms. Remove stems. Chop stems and add to bacon mixture. Fill mushrooms with bacon mixture. In 2-cup measure, heat bread crumbs and butter or margarine on High for 1 minute. Stir until well mixed. Press buttered crumbs on top of stuffed mushrooms. Place half the mushrooms in 6" x 10" baking dish, filling side up. Cook on High for 1 to 2 minutes. Repeat with remaining mushrooms. Makes about 50 stuffed mushrooms.

Bacon-Wrapped Water Chestnuts

A tempting blend of textures to make ahead and refrigerate.

1 (8-1/2-oz.) can water chestnuts, drained
8 slices bacon, cut in half
1/4 cup soy sauce

1/2 teaspoon ground ginger
1/2 teaspoon garlic salt

Wrap each water chestnut in half slice of bacon. Secure with toothpick. Combine remaining ingredients. Pour over bacon-wrapped water chestnuts. Refrigerate for several hours. Drain. Marinade can be stored in the refrigerator and reused. Place on metal rack in 7-1/2" x 12" utility dish. Cover with paper towel. Cook on High for 3 minutes. Turn dish. Cook 3 minutes more. Serve hot. Makes 16 appetizers.

Top to bottom: Cheese Puffs, Stuffed Mushrooms, Bacon-Wrapped Water Chestnuts.

Oysters-In-Shell

A delicate flavor enhanced by wine and garlic.

1 tablespoon butter
1/4 cup water
6 live oysters in shell

1/4 cup dry white wine
2 medium garlic cloves, finely chopped

In 2-quart casserole, melt butter with water and bring to boil on High for 1 minute. Arrange oysters evenly in casserole. Add wine and garlic. Cook, covered, on High for 3-1/2 minutes. Let stand, covered, 2 to 3 additional minutes or until shells open slightly. Open and serve on half-shell. Reserve liquid for dipping. Makes 1 to 2 servings.

Nachos

A hot and spicy instant appetizer.

1-8-oz. pkg. tortilla chips
1-1/2 cups grated Cheddar cheese
1 (4-oz.) can diced green chiles

1 (2-1/4-oz.) can sliced black olives
Red chile salsa

Empty chips onto serving platter. Cover with Cheddar cheese, then chilies and olives. Sprinkle with chile salsa. Heat for 3 to 4 minutes on Medium. Makes 4 to 6 servings.

Variation:
Sprinkle 1-1/2 cups grated Monterey Jack jalapeño pepper cheese over chips. Heat on Low for 2 minutes.

Vegetable Dip

Something for cheese and raw vegetable fans.

2 (4-1/2-oz.) pkgs. trimmed Brie cheese
1 (8-oz.) pkg. cream cheese
1 (2-in.) square sharp cheddar cheese slice

Brandy to taste
1/3 cup chopped walnuts

Put cheeses in 1-1/2-quart bowl. Melt on Low for 2 minutes, stirring often. Add brandy to taste and beat well. Fold in walnuts. Refrigerate overnight in a covered container. Place in dip bowl and serve with platter of fresh crisp vegetable dippers. Makes about 1-1/4 cups dip.

Tip   *To brown food, complete the required cooking time. Press the Browner button and set the timer for 3 to 5 minutes.*

Tortilla Foldovers

A flavor treat from the Southwest.

2 flour tortillas
Butter

Spread tortillas with butter. Fold in half and again in half, being careful not to crease or crack open the tortillas. Place on paper towel. Heat on High for 1 minute. Makes 2 foldovers.

Cocoa

An old-fashioned chocolate warm-up.

1/4 cup sugar
1/4 cup unsweetened powdered cocoa

1 cup water
3 cups milk

In 1-1/2-quart bowl, mix sugar with cocoa. Add water. Heat on High for 1-1/2 minutes, stirring once. Add milk. Heat on High for about 3 minutes or until piping hot, but not boiling. Makes 5 to 6 servings.

Hot Wine-Cranberry Punch

Burgundy adds zest to a cold-weather drink.

1 pt. cranberry-juice cocktail
1 cup water
3/4 cup sugar
2 sticks cinnamon

6 whole cloves
1 (4/5-qt.) bottle Burgundy wine
1 lemon, sliced

In 3-quart bowl, combine cranberry juice with water, sugar, cinnamon and cloves. Cover. Heat on High for 10 minutes. Strain. Pour strained cranberry mixture back into 3-quart bowl with wine and lemon. Heat on High for 5 minutes or until piping hot. Makes 12 to 15 cups of punch.

Mulled Cider

A hot, spicy treat for an Autumn day.

1 qt. cider
1/4 cup brown sugar, firmly packed
1 stick whole cinnamon

3 whole cloves
Orange slices

In 2-quart measuring cup or bowl, heat cider with sugar, cinnamon and cloves on High for 6 minutes. Strain and serve hot. Garnish with orange slices. Makes 4 servings.

Cappuccino

For sipping on a cold winter evening.

2 cups milk
4 teaspoons semi-sweet grated chocolate
4 teaspoons sugar
2 teaspoons instant-coffee powder

4 oz. brandy
Whipped cream
Grated chocolate

Heat milk in 4-cup glass measure on High for 3 minutes. Stir in chocolate, sugar and coffee. Pour into mugs. Add 1 ounce of brandy to each mug. Do not stir. Top with whipped cream and grated chocolate. Makes four 1/2-cup servings.

Mexican Chocolate

Olè! A rich blend of chocolate, coffee and spice.

2 cups milk
1/4 teaspoon ground cinnamon
2 oz. sweet cooking chocolate, chopped

2 teaspoons instant-coffee powder
1/4 cup whipping cream or whipped topping
2 teaspoons sugar (optional)

In 4-cup measure, heat milk and cinnamon on High about 4 minutes. Stir in chocolate and coffee. Heat on High for 30 seconds. Beat with rotary beater until frothy. Whip cream with sugar or use whipped topping. Pour hot chocolate into mugs; top with whipped cream or topping. Makes 2 servings.

Cappuccino

Tip *If you store food between 2 stapled paper plates, be sure to remove the staples before heating.*

Soups & Sandwiches

A soup and sandwich cooked in your microwave can be as elegant as a soup-to-nuts dinner or as hearty as a country supper, but a hundred times faster and easier!

French Onion Soup will please every connoisseur. Quick Burger Soup is easy and economical. Split-Pea Soup has the slow-cooked, old-fashioned flavor your family craves. Cook and serve soups in a tureen or casserole. There'll be no messy pots to wash. Or heat and serve soup in bowls or mugs. Stir soups occasionally while heating.

The flavor of sandwiches such as barbecued-beef, corned-beef or pastrami is improved with a microwave warm-up. Heat them on a napkin to absorb moisture. The top slice of bread won't become dry and tough if you open the sandwich and heat both halves simultaneously on Low. You can also heat sandwich fillings and spread them on buns or toast. Although the bread may be cool, the filling is hot. Let the sandwich stand briefly to distribute heat.

New England Clam Chowder

Microwave version of an old-fashioned favorite.

2 slices bacon, diced
1 medium onion, diced
2 medium potatoes, peeled and diced
2 (7-1/2-oz.) cans minced clams,
   drained; reserve liquid.
   Add water to make 2 cups liquid.

1/4 cup butter, melted
1/4 cup unsifted flour
3 cups milk
3/4 teaspoon salt
1/8 teaspoon pepper

In 3-quart casserole, cook bacon on High for 3 minutes. Add onion and potatoes. Cover. Cook on High for 5 minutes. Add clam juice and water. Cover. Cook on High for 8 to 10 minutes or until potatoes are tender. Melt butter in 2-cup liquid measure. Stir in flour and add to potato mixture, mixing well. Add clams and remaining ingredients. Cover. Cook on High for 4 to 5 minutes or until hot. Makes 4 to 6 servings.

New England Clam Chowder

Irish Country Soup

A quick treat for a cold evening.

1 (10-3/4-oz.) can cream-of-potato soup
1 (8-oz.) pkg. frozen green peas with
   cream sauce

1 chicken-bouillon cube
2 cups milk

In deep 1-1/2-quart bowl, combine soup, peas, bouillon and milk. Heat on High for 8 to 10 minutes or until bubbly hot, stirring often. Pour into blender. Blend until peas are broken up into small pieces. Makes 4 servings.

Oyster Stew

A tasty Christmas Eve tradition.

4 tablespoons butter
1 pint fresh oysters, drained;
   reserve liquor
1 (13-oz.) can evaporated milk
   and 13 oz. water

1/4 cup (approximately) oyster liquor
1/2 teaspoon salt
1/2 teaspoon pepper
Chopped chives

In 2-quart casserole, melt butter on High for 45 seconds. Add drained oysters. Cook on High until edges curl, about 4 to 5 minutes. Add milk, water, oyster liquor, salt and pepper. Cook on High 4 minutes longer, or almost to boiling point. Do not let milk boil. Garnish with chives. Makes 4 to 6 servings.

Tomato Consommé

Serve this at the start of an elegant dinner.

2-1/2 cups tomato juice
1 (10-oz.) can condensed consommé
1/4 teaspoon seasoned salt
1/4 teaspoon crumbled basil

1/4 teaspoon sugar
4 lemon slices
8 whole cloves

In 1-1/2-quart bowl, mix tomato juice with consommé, seasoned salt, basil and sugar. Stud lemon slices with cloves. Add to soup. Heat on High for 6 minutes. Makes 4 to 5 servings.

Tip   Don't use metal twist-ties on roasting bags. Use string, elastic or self-tie.

Cream-Of-Chicken Soup

Delicious, smooth and creamy.

6 tablespoons butter or margarine
1/3 cup flour
2 cups milk

2 cups chicken broth or bouillon
1/2 teaspoon seasoned salt
1 cup finely chopped cooked chicken

In 2-1/2-quart bowl, melt butter or margarine on High for 45 seconds. Stir in flour, then milk, broth and seasoned salt. Cook on High for 6 minutes, stirring often. Add chicken. Cook 1 minute. Makes 4 to 6 servings.

Curried Chicken Soup

A quick and spicy lunch.

1 (10-3/4-oz.) can cream-of-
   chicken soup, undiluted
1 soup-can milk
1/2 cup light cream

1 teaspoon curry powder
1 small apple, peeled and grated
1 teaspoon lemon juice
1 tablespoon chopped chives

In 2-quart bowl, combine all ingredients except chives. Cover. Cook on High for 5 minutes, stirring several times. Garnish with chives. Makes 4 servings.

French Onion Soup

Easy and authentic.

3 onions, thinly sliced
1/4 cup butter or margarine
4 cups beef broth or bouillon
1 teaspoon Worcestershire sauce

1/2 teaspoon salt
5 or 6 slices French bread, toasted
Grated Parmesan cheese

In covered 2-1/2-quart casserole, cook onions and butter or margarine on High for 10 minutes. Stir in broth, Worcestershire sauce and salt. Cover. Cook on High for another 5 minutes. Spoon into soup bowls suitable for use in a microwave oven (page 9.) Sprinkle toast with cheese. Float on top of soup. Heat on High for 30 seconds. Makes 5 to 6 servings.

 *Tip* *Use a pot holder to remove a dish from the oven when the Browner or Stay Hot has been on.*

Minestrone Soup

A complete meal in a soup bowl.

5 cups hot water
1 lb. beef shanks or stew meat
1 small onion, diced
1/4 teaspoon pepper
1/2 teaspoon basil
1/2 cup diced carrots
1 (1-lb.) can tomatoes

1/2 cup uncooked spaghetti, broken
    into 1-inch pieces
2 medium zucchini (3 to 4 inches long), sliced
1 (16-oz.) can kidney beans, drained
1 cup shredded cabbage
1 teaspoon salt
Grated Parmesan or Romano cheese

In 4-quart casserole, pour water over meat; add onion, pepper and basil. Cover. Cook on High for 25 minutes or until meat is tender, turning meat at least once. Remove meat from bone and cut into small pieces. Add meat to soup broth, along with carrots and tomatoes. Cover. Cook on High for 8 minutes. Stir in spaghetti, zucchini, beans, cabbage and salt. Cover. Cook on High for another 10 minutes, stirring once. Let stand, covered, several minutes. Sprinkle with cheese. Makes 6 servings.

Ham-Stuffed Rolls

A quick and hearty lunch.

2 cups finely chopped cooked ham
2 hard-cooked eggs, finely chopped
2 tablespoons minced green onion
2 tablespoons minced green pepper
1 teaspoon prepared mustard

1 tablespoon pickle relish
1/2 cup mayonnaise
4 large or 6 medium French rolls
1/2 cup shredded Cheddar cheese

Combine ham with eggs, onion, pepper, mustard, relish and mayonnaise. Cut off tops of rolls; scoop out. Fill with ham mixture. Sprinkle with cheese. Place in 7-1/2" x 12" baking dish. Cook on Medium for 3 minutes. Turn dish. Cook 2 minutes. Makes 4 to 6 sandwiches.

Minestrone Soup, Ham-Stuffed Rolls

Tip To keep food moist in the Stay Hot, cover it. Uncovered food will crisp under the Stay Hot.

Clam-Potato Chowder

A warm-up for a cold evening.

1 (10-3/4-oz.) can potato soup   Milk
1 (6-1/2-oz.) can minced clams, undrained   Dash of salt and pepper

Empty soup into a 4-cup measure. Drain clam juice into soup can. Set minced clams aside. Fill up can with milk and add to soup. Stir. Heat on Medium for 5 minutes, stirring once. Add clams. Heat through on High for 1-1/2 minutes. Add salt and pepper. Pour into soup mugs. Makes 4 servings.

Variation:
For thicker chowder, stir in 2 to 3 tablespoons of prepared instant potatoes before adding clams.

Split-Pea Soup

Hearty old-fashioned goodness.

1 cooked ham shank   1 small onion, chopped
2-1/2 quarts water   1 stalk celery, chopped
1 teaspoon salt   1 carrot, peeled and chopped
1/4 teaspoon pepper   1 lb. dried, split green peas

In 4-quart casserole, cover ham with water. Add salt, pepper, onion, celery, carrot and peas. Cover. Cook on High for 25 minutes. Remove ham shank from casserole; cut off any bits of ham. Add pieces of ham to soup broth. Cover. Cook on High for another 30 minutes or until peas are soft. Thicken with flour, if desired. For smoother consistency, puree soup in blender before serving. Makes 6 to 8 servings.

Quick Burger Soup

Cook this while your youngsters are coming to the table.

1/2 lb. lean ground beef   1 (10-1/2-oz.) can vegetable beef soup
1/4 teaspoon salt   1 cup water
1 teaspoon instant minced onion   1 (8-oz.) can tomato sauce

In 2-quart bowl, cook beef on High for 3 minutes, stirring once to break up chunks of meat. Pour off excess fat. Add salt, onion, soup, water and tomato sauce. Cook on High for 4 minutes. Serve with toasted buns. Makes 4 servings.

Tip   *Some recipes call for a metal meat rack in the utility dish. Be sure your brand of oven allows metal.*

Hot Reuben Sandwiches

A tasty blend of flavors with the tang of sauerkraut.

2 (3-oz.) pkgs. thin-sliced pressed ham shredded,
   or corn beef shredded
2 cups grated Swiss cheese (1/2 lb.)
1 cup Bavarian or regular sauerkraut,
   drained

3/4 teaspoon dill weed
1/2 cup Thousand Island dressing
8 to 12 slices dill-rye or rye bread

In 2-1/2-cup bowl, combine all ingredients, except bread. Toss lightly to mix and coat with dressing. Arrange 4 to 6 slices of bread (depending on size) on a serving platter. Spoon filling generously on each slice. Heat on Medium for 4 to 6 minutes or until cheese starts to melt. Top with remaining slices of bread. Heat on Medium for 1/2 to 1 minute or until bread is warm. Makes 4 to 6 servings.

Heat until cheese just starts to melt, top with remaining bread.

Meats & Poultry

Cooking meat in your microwave oven saves a lot of time and the results are tender and tasty.

Microwaves cook all surfaces of a doughnut-shaped food evenly. But because meat isn't doughnut-shaped, techniques and cooking times have to be adjusted to make up for its irregular shape.

The best technique is occasional turning to help the microwaves reach all the meat surfaces. See instructions in the meat-cooking tables for a particular cut of meat. Bones absorb microwaves and add to cooking time. Bone and roll meats for faster cooking.

Steaks, if they are 1-inch thick or more, can be cooked with good results with use of the Browner. Cook thinner steaks in a browning dish.

You may notice condensed moisture on the door of your microwave oven when you cook meat. This is normal and means the meat is cooking faster than the moisture can be expelled from the oven. Wipe it off with a paper towel.

Crisp meat by leaving it uncovered under the Stay Hot. If you want to keep the meat hot, but don't want it to crisp, cover it with foil. DO NOT use plastic wrap or paper under the Stay Hot.

Recipes and tables call for standing time after cooking. The internal temperature of meat increases by 10 to 15 degrees during standing time even though it's not exposed to heat. Time under the Browner or Stay Hot can be included in standing time. You may place a foil tent over the meat while it stands, with or without the Stay Hot. If you want to use your microwave to cook something else while the meat is standing, remove the meat from the microwave, cover with foil and set it anywhere out of drafts.

Read the cooking techniques at the front of each section before turning to the cooking table for detailed instructions. This will help you cook more efficiently.

BEEF- AND VEAL-COOKING TECHNIQUES

Preparation—Before cooking, season meats with onion powder, garlic powder, garlic cloves or seasoned blends. Salt draws out moisture if applied before cooking. You may prefer to salt afterwards or use other seasonings instead.

Shielding—Use foil over the less-thick parts to prevent overcooking. Cover shank ends or edges of an elongated roast with a smooth band of foil until halfway through the cooking time. *Leave more food uncovered than covered.* Use the least possible amount of foil to do the job.

Utensils—Use a metal rack in a utility dish if your oven allows use of metal. Use a rack designed and recommended for your oven brand. Cook less-tender meats in roasting bags or covered casseroles. Close roasting bags with string, a rubber band or a self-knot. DO NOT USE METAL TWIST-TIES. Make 6 knife slits in the bag before cooking.

Length of Cooking—Shape and tenderness affect cooking time. The larger around a roast is, the more minutes-per-pound it needs to cook and the lower the power level must be. Drain or siphon off excess fat halfway through the cooking time or more time will be needed. Less-tender meats are always cooked longer and slower, in a covered utensil. Turn the meat over halfway through the cooking time and rotate the dish back-to-front. See the meat table for cooking time.

Browning time depends on individual preference for color and crispness, but most meats brown in 5 to 7 minutes. **Do not use plastic or paper when using the Browner or Stay Hot.**

Test for Doneness—Insert a meat thermometer after roasting, unless you're using Thermador's Temp-Matic, or any oven with a temperature probe, or a microwave meat thermometer. A thermometer isn't reliable with less-tender meats because it can register well-done but the connective tissue will not be tenderized. For this reason the less-tender cuts have their own cooking table on page 76.

TEMPERATURE-TESTING BEEF AND VEAL

Doneness	Interior Temperature Before Standing		Interior Temperature After Standing 10 to 15 Minutes	
	°F	°C	°F	°C
Very Rare	110-115	43-46	125-130	52-54
Rare	120-125	49-52	135-140	57-60
Medium	130-135	54-57	145-150	63-66
Well Done	140-145	60-63	155-160	68-71

Cooking-time table, pages 74–76.
Temperature-probe table, page 24

Cooking and Standing—For a well-done, tender roast, use the Low setting while cooking. End slices are usually more done than the inner slices. Single servings can be cooked more by heating right on the plate.

During standing time, leave the meat in the microwave on Stay Hot or Brown, or remove it from the microwave and cover with foil.

LAMB-COOKING TECHNIQUES

Preparation—Roast lamb with or without bone. Shield the shank end or less-thick ends with smoothly fitted foil for half the cooking time. Insert garlic slivers into the meat or use seasoned salt or herbs.

Utensil—Place lamb on the metal rack in the utility dish if metal is allowed in your oven. Because lamb is a tender meat, you don't have to cover it. A paper towel laid over the roast will absorb most of the spatter, but let the steam escape.

Length of Cooking—Lamb with bone-in will take about 1 to 1-1/2 minutes-per-pound longer to cook than without the bone. The cooking times offer a choice in doneness because lamb doesn't need to be well done. The Medium setting requires less time but more turning. The Low setting requires longer cooking time but the meat needs to be turned only once. Choose the method that suits you best. Remember to drain or siphon fat out of the dish at the halfway point to avoid extending the cooking time.

Test for Doneness—Insert a meat thermometer after roasting, unless you're using Thermador's Temp-Matic, any oven with a temperature probe, or a microwave meat thermometer.

TEMPERATURE-TESTING LAMB

Doneness	Interior Temperature Before Standing		Interior Temperature After Standing 10 to 15 Minutes	
	°F	°C	°F	°C
Medium	140	60	155	68
Well Done	155-160	68-71	170-180	77-82

Cooking-time table, page 79.
Temperature-probe table, page 24.

Tip *Heat brandy for flaming foods on High for 15 seconds. Ignite and pour over food.*

PORK-COOKING TECHNIQUES

Preparation—Season pork with garlic slivers, seasoned powders or herbs. Select a pork roast as symetrically shaped as possible, with or without bones. Use foil to shield the bones.

Utensil—Roast pork on a metal rack in the utility dish if metal is allowed in your oven. Drain or siphon the fat once during cooking. Cook pork chops in a browning dish, on a meat rack or directly on a heat-resistant platter or utility dish.

Length of Cooking—Use the Low setting to cook even tender cuts of pork roasts. Cook them through, but don't cook pork until it's dried out. Although the quality controls for pork are much improved, pork should be cooked just to an interior temperature of 160°F (71°C) to safeguard against the possible presence of the trichinosis parasite. If you have no way of checking the internal temperature, eliminate the danger by storing pork in the freezer for 2 or 3 weeks before cooking.

Test for Doneness—Insert a meat thermometer after roasting, unless you're using Thermador's Temp-Matic, any oven with a temperature probe, or a microwave meat thermometer.

TEMPERATURE-TESTING PORK					
Doneness	Interior Temperature Before Standing		Interior Temperature After Standing 10 to 15 Minutes		
	°F	°C	°F	°C	
Well	160	71	170	77	

Cooking-time table, page 77.
Temperature-probe table, page 24.

HAM-COOKING TECHNIQUES

Preparation—Choose a ham as evenly shaped as possible. With irregular shapes, such as a canned ham or the shank end of a ham, use foil for shielding. Fit the foil smoothly on the small end of the ham at the start of cooking and remove it halfway through the cooking time. Score the ham at the start and brush with glaze after turning over. If the ham has a rind, leave it on until the last 15 minutes. Then remove the rind along with most of the fat and brush with glaze.

Utensil—Place the ham on a metal meat rack in a utility dish if metal is allowed in your oven. Lay wax paper over the ham to help hold in the heat during cooking.

Length of Cooking—Most hams and ham steaks are purchased precooked, so you'll heat ham *just to serving temperature.* The high sugar and fat content in ham cause it to heat quickly.

Test for Doneness—Insert a meat thermometer after roasting, unless you're using Thermador's Temp-Matic, any oven with a temperature probe, or a microwave meat thermometer. During standing time, cover with foil and place under Stay Hot.

TEMPERATURE-TESTING HAM					
Type	Interior Temperature Before Standing		Interior Temperature After Standing 10 to 15 Minutes		
	°F	°C	°F	°C	
Fully Cooked	95-115	46	130	54	
Uncooked	150	66	160	71	

Cooking-time table, page 78.
Temperature-probe table, page 24.

Tip To soften raisins or other dried fruit, add 1 to 3 teaspoons of water or other liquid and cover. Heat on High for 15 to 30 seconds. Let stand 2 to 3 minutes. Drain.

POULTRY-COOKING TECHNIQUES

Preparation—Giblets require long, slow cooking, so cook them conventionally. Wash the poultry and dry well with paper towels. Stuff the bird just before cooking. Truss whole birds with wet string to hold in legs and wings. Cook poultry parts plain or coated with herbed flour or crumbs. To baste the skin, use unsalted or sweet butter. Salt draws moisture to the skin which toughens and blisters it.

Utensils—Put poultry on a metal meat rack in a utility dish if metal is allowed in your oven. Cook large birds in a paper shopping bag. When you steam poultry in a plastic roasting bag, use a shorter cooking time and tie the bag with string—DO NOT USE A METAL TWIST TIE.

Length of Cooking—You'll find 2 time settings on the poultry-cooking table, pages 79 and 80. The slower time makes poultry slightly more moist. You may prefer to cook it faster. Cooking times vary for several reasons: age of bird, diet, amount of time in storage and temperature before cooking. The preferred size for a large bird is 10 to 12 pounds. Turn the bird twice during cooking because of its irregular shape and the amount of bone.

Test for Doneness—When cooking stuffed poultry, insert a microwave thermometer in the center of the stuffing and cook until the temperature reaches 155°F (68°C). After standing time, the thermometer should read 165°F (74°C). Turkey breast is cooked to 155°F (68°C), with a temperature of 170°F (77°C) after standing.

Do not use a thermometer in an unstuffed turkey or chicken because the reading won't be accurate.

When you can't use a meat thermometer, test by moving a drumstick up and down. The joint should move freely. You can also pierce the inside of the thigh with a fork. The juices should be clear, with no sign of pink. These tests should be done *after* standing time.

Beef-Filled Squash

The flavors blend for a new taste.

2 medium acorn squash	1 lb. lean ground beef
4 slices bacon, diced	1/2 teaspoon salt
1/4 cup chopped onion	1/4 cup fine, dry bread crumbs
1/2 teaspoon salt	1 tablespoon butter or margarine

Cook whole squash on paper towels on High for 8 to 9 minutes or until soft. Let stand for 5 minutes. In 2-quart casserole, cook bacon and onion on High for 3 minutes. Add 1/2 teaspoon salt and meat. Cook on High for 4 to 5 minutes, stirring often. Cut cooked squash lengthwise; discard seeds and fibers. Carefully remove squash from shells; reserve shells. In small bowl, whip squash with 1/2 teaspoon salt until squash is fluffy. Combine with the meat mixture. Return to squash shells. Measure bread crumbs into 1-cup measure; add butter or margarine. Heat on High for 1 minute. Stir well. Raise shelf. Cook stuffed shells on Medium for 3 minutes. Top with bread crumb mixture and brown for 5 minutes. Makes 4 servings.

See Meat Cooking Tables, pages 73 to 80.

43

Stuffed Flank Steak

A superb gourmet dinner topped with savory sauce.

3/4 cup packaged bread stuffing
1 (3-oz.) can sliced mushrooms, drained
2 tablespoons melted butter or margarine
1 tablespoon grated Parmesan cheese
1 flank steak (about 1-3/4 lbs.),
   tenderized

1 (3/4-oz.) pkg. brown-gravy mix
1/4 cup dry red wine
2 tablespoons minced green onions
1 tablespoon salad oil
1 garlic clove
1/4 cup currant jelly

Combine bread stuffing with mushrooms, butter or margarine and cheese. Spread over flank steak; roll up like jelly roll. Fasten with wooden skewers. Prepare gravy mix according to package directions. Heat on High for 4-1/2 to 5-1/2 minutes, stirring once. Add wine and onions. Pour oil in 7-1/2" x 12" utility dish with garlic clove. Heat on High for 2 minutes. Remove clove. Roll steak in oil, coating all sides. Pour gravy, wine and onions over meat. Cover with plastic wrap. Cook on Low for 35 minutes, turn meat over half way through cooking time. Brown 6 minutes. Let stand 5 minutes. Remove meat from sauce; add jelly. Heat on High for 2 minutes until jelly is dissolved. Serve sauce over meat. Makes 4 to 6 servings.

Swiss Steak in a Roasting Bag

A family favorite made in half the time with half the effort.

1-1/2 lbs. thick round steak
1/4 cup flour
1 (1-oz.) pkg. seasoning mix for Swiss steak

1 (8-oz.) can tomato sauce
1/2 cup water

Cut steak into serving-size pieces. Coat with flour. Place in single layer in roasting bag. In a 2-cup measure, combine package of seasoning mix, tomato sauce and water. Heat on High for 4 minutes. Pour over steak in bag. Close bag with string or rubber band and place in 7-1/2" x 12" utility dish. Puncture 4 holes in top of bag. Allow to marinate 10 minutes. Cook on Low for 25 minutes. Let stand 10 minutes. Makes 4 to 5 servings.

Tip   *Melt 2 tablespoons of butter in a glass measuring cup on High for 15 seconds. Melt 1/4 cup in 30 seconds.*

Cheese-Stuffed Burgers

Cheese sauce covers hamburgers stuffed with mushrooms and onions.

3/4 cups Basic Creamy-Sauce Mix, page 128
1-1/4 cups milk
1-1/2 cups (6-oz.) grated sharp process
   American cheese
1 egg, slightly beaten

1 cup soft bread crumbs
1 lb. lean ground beef
1 (3-oz.) can chopped mushrooms, drained
1/2 cup cooked rice
1 tablespoon chopped green onion

In 4-cup measure, combine sauce mix with milk. Cook on High for 2 to 2-1/2 minutes or until thick and bubbly, stirring once. Add cheese and mix until cheese is melted. In medium mixing bowl, combine egg, 1/3 cup of the cooked sauce and bread crumbs. Mix in ground beef. Shape into 4 circles, each circle 6 inches in diameter. Combine 1/4 cup of the mushrooms, all of the rice and green onions. Spoon 2 tablespoons of mushroom mixture into center of each meat circle. Fold edges of circles over stuffing and seal. Cook in 7-1/2" x 12" utility dish on High for 5 to 6 minutes, turning burgers over halfway through cooking. Add the rest of the mushrooms to remaining cheese sauce and pour over burgers. Heat on High for 1-1/2 minutes. Spoon sauce over burgers before serving. Makes 4 servings.

French Stuffed Hamburgers

Roquefort provides a gourmet touch.

1 lb. lean ground beef
6 to 8 fresh mushrooms, washed and sliced
4 teaspoons Roquefort cheese, crumbled

Salt
Worcestershire sauce
5 to 6 teaspoons soy sauce

Divide the meat into 8 patties, each one 4 inches in diameter. Top 4 patties with mushrooms and 1 teaspoon Roquefort cheese on each. Salt each patty. Add a dash of Worcestershire sauce and 1 teaspoon soy sauce to each. Cover with a second patty. Seal edges, enclosing the mushroom mixture. Place on metal rack in 7-1/2" x 12" utility dish. Brush with soy sauce. Cook on High for 2 minutes. Turn patties over. Brush again with soy sauce. Cook on High for 2-1/2 minutes. Brown 4 to 6 minutes. Makes 4 servings.

Tip *If everyone arrives home for dinner at a different time, arrange individual servings on dinner plates. Cover. Heat each plate as needed.*

Basic Meatballs

Plan ahead for a meal in a minute.

3 eggs
1/2 cup milk
3 cups soft bread crumbs
1/2 cup finely chopped onion

1 tablespoon oregano
2 teaspoons salt
3 lbs. ground beef

In large mixing bowl, beat eggs. Stir in milk, bread crumbs, onion, oregano and salt. Add meat and mix well. Shape into 72 meatballs 1-inch thick. Arrange in large tray; slip tray in plastic bag and tie. Freeze until firm. Repackage in freezer bags, using 24 meatballs per bag. Tie and freeze. Makes 72 meatballs.

Chinese Meatballs

Flavorful meatballs with a crunchy texture.

1-1/2 lbs. ground beef
3/4 cup minced celery
1/2 cup soft bread crumbs
1/4 cup chopped almonds
1 large egg

1 tablespoon soy sauce
1 garlic clove, minced
1 teaspoon salt
1/2 teaspoon MSG
Sweet-Sour Sauce, page 126

Mix ingredients thoroughly. Form into small meatballs the size of walnuts. Place on the metal meat rack in a 7-1/2" x 12" utility dish, allowing space around each meatball. Cover with paper towel. Cook on High for 5 to 7 minutes. Brown for 6 minutes. Serve with Sweet-Sour Sauce, page 126, as an appetizer or main course. Makes 4 to 6 servings.

Teriyaki Beef and Bacon

Browning improves the Teriyaki flavor.

8 slices bacon
1 lb. lean ground beef
1/4 cup soy sauce
2 tablespoons lemon juice

2 tablespoons honey
2 tablespoons white wine
1 garlic clove
1/4 teaspoon ground ginger

Place bacon on metal rack in 7-1/2" x 12" utility dish. Cook on High for 2 minutes. Form beef into 4 patties. Wrap each patty in 2 slices of bacon. Secure with toothpicks. Place in shallow dish. Combine remaining ingredients, pour over meat and refrigerate several hours. Drain. Place on metal rack in 7-1/2" x 12" utility dish. Cook on High for 5 to 6 minutes or until done. Raise shelf. Brown for 4 minutes. Makes 4 servings.

Swiss Steak

Rich and delicious tomato-cheese combination.

2 lbs. round steak, 1/2-inch thick
1/4 cup flour
1 teaspoon salt
1/8 teaspoon pepper
3 tablespoons shortening
1 onion, sliced
1/2 teaspoon oregano, crushed
1/4 teaspoon garlic powder

1/2 cup chopped celery
1/2 green pepper, chopped
1 (28-oz.) can tomatoes,
   mashed, do not drain
1/4 cup water
1/2 teaspoon salt
1/4 lb. mozzarella cheese,
   thinly sliced (optional)

Pound meat with meat mallet to tenderize. Dredge meat in mixture of flour, 1 teaspoon salt and pepper. On cooktop, heat shortening in a 4-quart glass-ceramic casserole. Add meat. Brown both sides. Cook onions until transparent. Stir in remaining ingredients including flour mixture, except cheese. Be sure all the meat is covered with liquid. Cover and cook on Low for 45 minutes or until meat is tender, stirring every 15 minutes. Top meat with cheese slices. Makes 4 to 6 servings.

Meat Loaf

Subtle seasonings give an old favorite new life.

TO MAKE 4 SERVINGS:
1 lb. lean ground beef
1 egg
1/2 cup Italian-seasoned bread crumbs;
  use plain crumbs, if desired
1/4 cup milk
1/2 cup diced Swiss cheese
2 tablespoons catsup
2 tablespoons dry onion-soup mix
2 tablespoons soy sauce

TO MAKE 6 TO 8 SERVINGS:
2 lbs. lean ground beef
1 egg
1 cup Italian-seasoned bread crumbs;
  use plain crumbs, if desired
1/2 cup milk
1 cup diced Swiss cheese
4 tablespoons catsup
3 tablespoons dry onion-soup mix
3 tablespoons soy sauce

Combine all the ingredients and put in a loaf-shaped baking dish, or form by hand into a loaf and place in 2-quart casserole. For a 1-pound meat loaf, cook on Medium for 12 to 14 minutes. For a 2-pound meat loaf, cook on Medium for 20 to 22 minutes. Brown 5 minutes.

Swiss Steak

Tip Cook food the minimum suggested cooking time. A few seconds of overcooking can dry out food.

Individual Meat Loaves

A new size disguises an old favorite.

1/2 cup soft bread crumbs
1/2 cup evaporated milk
2 eggs, slightly beaten
1 teaspoon salt
1/8 teaspoon pepper
1 small onion, finely chopped

1/4 teaspoon ground thyme
1-1/2 lbs. lean ground beef
1/4 lb. process American cheese
3/4 cup chili sauce
1 tablespoon Worcestershire sauce
1 teaspoon prepared mustard

In mixing bowl, combine bread crumbs, milk, eggs, salt, pepper, onion and thyme. Add meat; mix well. Cut cheese into 6 cubes. Divide meat into 6 equal portions and form around cheese cubes to make small loaves. Place in 7-1/2" x 12" utility dish. Cover with wax paper. Cook on High for 4 minutes. Turn dish. Cook another 4 minutes. Drain fat. Combine chili sauce, Worcestershire sauce and mustard. Pour over meat. Cook, uncovered, on High for 2 minutes. Makes 6 servings.

Basic Meat Sauce

Keep a supply of this versatile sauce in your freezer.

3 lbs. lean ground beef
2 medium onions, chopped
2 garlic cloves, minced
3/4 cup finely chopped celery
1 (28-oz.) can tomatoes, cut up
3 (6-oz.) cans tomato paste
1 cup beef bouillon

2 tablespoons minced parsley
1 tablespoon Worcestershire sauce
1 teaspoons salt
1 teaspoon brown sugar
1/2 teaspoon pepper
1 bay leaf

In 4-quart casserole, combine beef with onions, garlic and celery. Cover. Cook on High for 10 minutes, stirring twice. Drain excess fat. Add remaining ingredients. Cover. Cook on High for 20 minutes, stirring twice. Add all or part of sauce to main dishes or freeze for future use. Freeze in 1-quart units in freezer cartons or jars. Thaw before using in recipes. Makes about 3 quarts.

Meat and Potato Pie

Tangy meat and potatoes make a scrumptious supper.

1 egg, beaten
3/4 cup soft bread crumbs
1/2 cup milk
1/4 teaspoon salt
Dash pepper
1 lb. lean ground beef.

1/2 cup chopped green onion
1/3 cup chili sauce
1 teaspoon prepared mustard
3 cups cooked, diced potatoes
1/2 cup grated sharp Cheddar cheese

Combine egg, bread crumbs, milk, salt and pepper. Add beef and mix well. Press into bottom and sides of 9-inch pie plate. Cook on High for 3 minutes. Combine onion, chili sauce and mustard. Pour over potatoes and toss lightly. Spoon into baked meat shell. Raise shelf. Cook on High for 3 minutes. Sprinkle with cheese. Brown for 4 minutes. Makes 4 servings.

Veal Chop Suey

A tasty budget-stretcher.

3 tablespoons butter or margarine
2 cups thinly sliced veal
2 tablespoons flour
1-1/2 cups diced celery
1 cup chopped onions
1 teaspoon salt
1/8 teaspoon pepper

1 cup chicken bouillon
1 cup bean sprouts
1/2 cup canned mushroom pieces
1 tablespoon soy sauce
1 tablespoon Worcestershire sauce
2 tablespoons cornstarch
1/2 cup cold water

Melt butter or margarine in 4-quart casserole on High for 35 seconds. Dip veal in flour; add to butter. Cook on High 4 to 5 minutes, stirring once. Stir in celery, onions, salt, pepper and bouillon. Cook on High for 8 minutes. Add bean sprouts, mushrooms, soy sauce and Worcestershire sauce. Dissolve cornstarch in cold water. Stir into meat mixture. Cook on High for 4 minutes. Serve with rice or noodles. Makes 4 to 6 servings.

Veal Scaloppine

Old-country flavor but quick and easy.

1 lb. thin veal cutlets
1/4 cup flour
1/4 cup butter or margarine
1 garlic clove, minced
4 large fresh mushrooms, sliced

1/4 cup dry white wine
1 chicken-bouillon cube
1/4 cup hot water
Salt and pepper

Cut veal into serving-size pieces. Coat with flour. In 7-1/2" x 12" utility dish, melt butter or margarine with garlic on High for 1 minute. Coat meat with butter or margarine mixture. Cook on High for 2 minutes. Stir. Cook on High for another 2 minutes. Add mushrooms, wine and bouillon dissolved in hot water. Cover with wax paper. Cook on High 2 minutes more. Add salt and pepper to taste. Makes 4 servings.

Liver and Onions

Good, and good for you!

4 slices bacon
1 medium onion, sliced

1 lb. baby-beef liver, sliced
Salt and pepper

Put bacon on the metal rack in the 7-1/2" x 12" utility dish. Cook on High for 3 to 4 minutes. Cover with paper towel to catch spatters. Remove bacon and metal rack. Set bacon aside to crisp. Add onion slices to bacon drippings in dish; stir to coat. Cook on High for 3 to 4 minutes until light brown, stirring once. Push onions aside. Add liver, coating with drippings. Season with salt and pepper. Put onions on top of liver slices. Crumble bacon and sprinkle on top of onions. Cover with wax paper. Cook on High for 2-1/2 to 3-1/2 minutes until pink color is barely gone. Turn dish and rearrange liver slices once. Brown as desired. Makes 4 servings.

Freezer-to-Table Pot Roast

The ultimate in convenience.

1 (3-lb.) beef chuck roast, completely frozen
1 (1-1/4 to 1-1/2 oz.) envelope
   dry onion-soup mix
1 lb. (4 small) new potatoes, peeled
   and quartered

1 cup sliced celery, cut 1-inch thick
2 cups slivered carrots, cut 2-inches long
1 cup thinly sliced onions,
   separated into rings

Place completely frozen meat in 4-quart casserole. Cover tightly. Cook on Low for 30 minutes. Turn over and sprinkle with 1/2 the onion-soup mix. Cover. Cook on Low for an additional 30 minutes. Turn meat over again and sprinkle with remaining onion-soup mix. Add vegetables around meat with onion rings on top. Cover. Cook on Low for 20 to 30 minutes until meat and vegetables are tender. Let stand, covered, 10 minutes. Makes 4 to 6 servings.

Place frozen meat in cooking dish, cover tightly and cook for 1/3 the time. Turn roast and sprinkle with 1/2 of onion-soup mix. After approximately 2/3 of cooking time, turn roast over again, add remaining soup mix and vegetables, return to oven and finish cooking.

Freezer-to-Table Swiss Steak

Defrost and cook in about an hour.

2 lbs. beef round steak, completely frozen
1 (1-oz.) pkg. Swiss-steak seasoning

1 (4-oz.) can mushrooms, stems and
    pieces, drained

Use casserole size closest to shape of meat. In a 2 to 3-quart covered casserole, cook meat on Low for 15 minutes. Drain liquid. Turn meat over. Add packaged seasoning and mushrooms. Cover. Cook on Low for 30 to 40 minutes or until tender. Let stand, covered, for 5 minutes. Makes 4 servings.

Freezer-to-Table Rump Roast

A real time-saver.

1 (3-lb.) rump roast, completely frozen
1 (1-1/2-oz.) pkg. dry gravy mix
2 small onions

6 stalks celery, coarsely sliced
6 carrots, cut lengthwise and halved

Put meat in 4-quart casserole and cover. Cook on Low for 30 minutes. Drain liquid. Turn meat over. Sprinkle with dry gravy-mix. Add vegetables over and around meat. Cover. Cook on Low for 25 to 30 minutes or until fork tender. Let stand, covered, for 10 minutes. Makes 6 servings.

Tip   Pierce plastic wrap to allow steam to escape from tightly wrapped or covered foods.

Minted Lamb Chops

Tender lamb in savory mint sauce.

1/2 cup wine vinegar
1/2 cup apple-mint jelly
2 tablespoons brown sugar
1 tablespoon lemon juice
1 teaspoon grated lemon peel

1/2 teaspoon dry mustard
6 loin lamb chops (about 2 lbs.),
   1-inch thick
Salt and pepper

In 4-cup measure, combine vinegar, jelly, sugar, lemon juice, lemon peel and mustard. Heat on High for 2 minutes or until jelly melts, stirring once. Cool slightly; pour over lamb chops. Marinate several hours. Drain and reserve marinade. Place lamb chops on metal rack in 7-1/2" x 12" utility dish. Brush with marinade. Raise shelf. Cook on High for 4 minutes. Turn chops and brush with marinade. Cook on High for 5 minutes. Sprinkle with salt and pepper. Brown 5 minutes. Makes 3 servings.

Lemon-Butter Glazed Lamb Roast

With melt-in-your-mouth tenderness, this roast will disappear fast.

1 (5-lb.) lamb roast, boned
Freshly ground pepper
1 teaspoon ground oregano
3 garlic cloves

1/4 cup butter
1/3 cup lemon juice
1 teaspoon soy sauce

Sprinkle all sides of lamb with pepper and oregano. Cut 1 garlic clove and rub over roast. Crush remaining garlic. In 1-cup measure melt butter on High for 40 seconds. Add lemon juice, soy sauce and remaining garlic. Place roast, skin side down, on metal rack in 7-1/2" x 12" utility dish. Pour half the glaze over meat. Cook on Medium for 12 minutes. Turn dish. Cook a second 12 minutes. Turn roast over. Protect edges and small end from overcooking with small pieces of foil. Pour remaining glaze over meat. Cook on Medium for a final 12 minutes. Turn dish. Cook 14 minutes. Brown 4 to 5 minutes. Remove from oven. Cover with foil and let stand 20 minutes. Makes about 6 servings.

Rio Grande Pork Roast

An unusual flavor blend gives pork pizzaz.

1/2 teaspoon salt
1/2 teaspoon garlic salt
1/2 teaspoon chili powder
1/4 teaspoon liquid smoke
1 (5-lb.) pork-loin roast, boned and tied

1/2 cup apple jelly
1/2 cup catsup
1 tablespoon vinegar
1/2 teaspoon chili powder
1 cup crushed corn chips

Combine the salt, garlic salt and 1/2 teaspoon chili powder. Rub liquid smoke over roast and sprinkle with mixture of seasonings. Shield ends of roast with foil for first half of roasting. Apply foil as smoothly as possible. In a 2-cup glass measure, combine jelly, catsup, vinegar and 1/2 teaspoon chili powder. Heat to boiling on High for about 3-1/2 to 4-1/2 minutes. Stir and set aside. Place roast in utility dish. Cook, fat side down, on Low for 40 minutes. Remove foil and turn roast, fat side up. Brush generously with glaze. Sprinkle with corn chips. Cook on Low for 30 to 35 minutes more. Internal temperature should register 150°F (66°C) to 160°F (71°C) immediately after cooking. Temperature increases to 170°F (77°C) after 15 minutes standing time. Roast can be browned during part of standing time or kept warm on Stay Hot for 15 minutes. Excellent served with rice. Makes 8 to 10 servings.

Glazed Pork Roast

Serve yams or sweet potatoes with this fruit-glazed roast.

1 tablespoon cornstarch
1 tablespoon lemon juice
1 (8-oz.) can crushed pineapple,
   not drained
1 cup apricot nectar

2 tablespoons soy sauce
1 tablespoon corn syrup
4-lb. pork-loin roast, boned
Salt and pepper

In 4-cup measure, dissolve cornstarch in lemon juice. Stir in undrained pineapple, apricot nectar, soy sauce and corn syrup. Cook on High for 4 minutes, stirring twice. Set aside. Place roast, fat side down, on metal rack in 7-1/2" x 12" utility dish. Brush with sauce and cover with wax paper. Cook on Medium for 9 minutes. Give dish a half turn. Cook for a second 9 minutes. Turn roast fat side up and brush with sauce. Cook on Medium for a third 9 minutes. Sprinkle with salt and pepper. Give dish a half turn again. Cook on Medium for a final 9 minutes. Brush with sauce. Brown 5 minutes. Let stand 10 minutes before carving. Serve with extra sauce. Makes 4 to 6 servings.

Pork Hawaiian

This exotic combination goes together quickly.

3 cups cubed cooked pork
  (about 1-1/2 lbs.)
1/3 cup brown sugar, firmly packed
2 tablespoons cornstarch
1/2 teaspoon ground ginger
1/4 teaspoon garlic powder
1/4 cup soy sauce
2 tablespoons catsup
1 onion, cut in chunks

1 green pepper, cubed
1 (20-oz.) can pineapple chunks
  packed in pineapple juice
1/3 cup wine vinegar
1/4 cup soy sauce
1 tablespoon cornstarch
1 (8-oz.) can water chestnuts, drained
1 (3-oz.) jar sliced mushrooms

Place pork cubes in a 2-1/2-quart glass-ceramic casserole. Combine brown sugar, cornstarch, ginger and garlic powder in a 2-cup liquid measure. Stir in soy sauce and catsup. Pour over pork. Stir to coat all of pork. Cook on High for 3 minutes. Add onion and green pepper. Cook on High for 4 minutes. Drain pineapple, reserving juice. To pineapple juice add water to make 1 cup of liquid. Add vinegar and soy sauce. Stir in cornstarch. Pour over cooked pork. Cook on High for 6 to 7 minutes until sauce is thick. Add water chestnuts, pineapple chunks and mushrooms. Continue to cook on High for 2 to 3 minutes. Serve over hot rice. Makes 6 to 8 servings.

Pork Chops with Scalloped Potatoes

The secret is to slice the potatoes very thin.

1 (10-3/4-oz.) can cream-of-mushroom soup
1/3 cup milk
3 large potatoes, peeled and thinly
  sliced (1-1/4 lbs.)
1/2 to 1 small onion, thinly sliced

Salt and pepper
4 pork chops (1 lb.)
Garlic salt
Seasoned salt

In 4-cup measure, heat soup and milk on High for 4 minutes. Stir. In a 7-1/2" x 12" utility dish, layer potatoes and onion, salt and pepper. Pour hot soup mixture over all and cover with plastic wrap. Cook on High for 10 minutes until potatoes are crisp-tender. Lightly sprinkle pork chops with blend of garlic salt and seasoned salt. Add pork chops to potatoes, placing tenderloin side towards center. Cover. Cook on High for about 4 minutes. Remove cover. Raise shelf. Brown for 6 minutes. Makes 4 servings.

Pork Hawaiian

Tip

To soften frozen-juice concentrates, remove one end of the can and heat in the opened can on High for 30 seconds. Let stand 3 to 5 minutes and add water.

Calico Stuffed Peppers

Colorful and spicy.

3 large green peppers	3 tablespoons catsup
1 lb. bulk sausage	1/4 teaspoon garlic salt
3/4 cup chopped onion	1 (8-oz.) can tomato sauce
1 (8-oz.) can whole-kernel corn, drained	1/2 cup grated Cheddar cheese

Wash peppers and cut in half lengthwise. Cut stems; scoop out seeds. In covered 4-quart casserole, cook peppers on High for 4 minutes. In 2-quart casserole, cook sausage and onion on High for 5 minutes, stirring once. Drain excess fat. Stir in corn, catsup and garlic salt. Spoon mixture into peppers. Return stuffed peppers to 4-quart casserole. Pour tomato sauce over all. Cover. Cook on High for 5 minutes. Sprinkle with cheese. Cook, uncovered, for 1 additional minute. Makes 6 servings.

Variation:

Italian sausage may also be used, or try 1/2 pound lean ground beef and 1/2 pound sausage.

Sauces & Glazes to Serve with Ham

Follow directions on Ham Cooking Table, page 78, for baking ham. Use any of the following glazes or sauces.

Strawberry Sauce

Fruit'n spice and everything nice.

1 (10-oz.) pkg. frozen strawberries	Dash cinnamon
1 tablespoon cornstarch	Dash ground cloves

Open one end of the strawberry package. Place the package on a paper towel. Heat on High for 1 to 1-1/2 minutes to thaw slightly. Pour into 4-cup measure and stir in the remaining ingredients. Cook on High for 3 minutes or until translucent, stirring twice. Baste ham while it is cooking. Serve ham with extra sauce. Makes approximately 2/3 cup of sauce.

Variation:

Substitute frozen raspberries for strawberries.

Honey and Marmalade Glaze

An easy dress-up for canned ham.

2 tablespoons honey
1/4 cup orange, lime, or lemon marmalade

Place honey and marmalade in 1-cup measure and heat on High for 1-1/2 minutes; stir. Baste ham while it is cooking. Serve ham with extra glaze. Makes 1/4 cup of glaze.

Apricot-Ginger Sauce

Baste an old favorite with a different touch.

1/2 cup brown sugar, firmly packed
1 tablespoon cornstarch
1 (12-oz.) can apricot nectar

1 tablespoon lemon juice
1/2 teaspoon ginger

In 4-cup measure, combine brown sugar and cornstarch. Stir in the remaining ingredients. Heat on High for 4 minutes or until translucent, stirring twice. Baste ham while it is cooking. Serve ham with extra sauce. Makes 3/4 cup of sauce.

Holiday Glaze and Sauce

Adds shimmery elegance to baked ham.

Glaze:
3/4 cup red-currant jelly
1/4 cup cranberry juice
2 tablespoons lemon juice

1 teaspoon grated orange peel
1/8 teaspoon nutmeg
Whole cloves

Sauce:
2 tablespoons cornstarch
1/2 cup cranberry juice

2 tablespoons orange juice
3 tablespoons lemon juice
2/3 of glaze

Glaze:
Combine glaze ingredients in 4-cup measure. Heat on High for 1-1/2 to 2 minutes, stirring once. Score ham in diamond design and stud with cloves. Use 1/3 of the glaze for basting. Use the remainder for the sauce. Makes approximately 1 cup of glaze.

Sauce:
Place the cornstarch in a 2-cup measure and slowly add the cranberry juice, stirring constantly. Add the orange juice, lemon juice and remainder of glaze. Heat on High for 3 minutes or until sauce is translucent, stirring twice. Makes approximately 3/4 cup of sauce.

Oriental Ham Kabobs

Island flavors with a snappy sauce.

1 green pepper
1 (14-oz.) can pineapple chunks, drained; reserve 1/4 cup syrup
1 lb. cooked ham, cut into 1-inch cubes

Plum Sauce:

1 (1 lb.) can purple plums, drained
3/4 cup sugar
2 tablespoons cornstarch
1/3 cup vinegar

1/4 cup pineapple syrup from canned pineapple
2 teaspoons dry minced onion
1/2 teaspoon salt

Wash pepper and cut in half lengthwise. Cut stem; scoop out seeds. Place on paper towel and partially cook on High for 1-1/2 minutes. Cube. Drain pineapple chunks, reserving syrup. Thread ham, pineapple and green pepper on wooden skewers. Brush kabobs with plum sauce. Raise shelf. Cook on High for 2 minutes. Brown for 3-1/2 minutes. Turn kabobs over. Brush with more sauce. Brown for 3 to 4 minutes. Makes 4 servings.

Plum sauce:
Pit plums and puree in blender. Blend sugar with cornstarch. In 4-cup measure, add to vinegar, pineapple juice, onion and salt. Cook on High for 5 minutes, stirring twice. Mix in pureed plums.

Bavarian Pork Chops

A flavor that's easy on the cook.

1 (1-lb.) can sauerkraut, drained
1/4 teaspoon caraway seeds
1 cooking apple, cored, peeled and grated

4 loin or rib pork chops (1-1/2 to 2 lbs.)
Salt and pepper

In bottom of 7-1/2" x 12" utility dish, combine sauerkraut with caraway seeds and apple. Top with pork chops. Cover with wax paper. Cook on Medium for 4 to 5 minutes and turn chops. Cook another 4 to 5 minutes. Sprinkle with salt and pepper. Makes 6 servings.

Oriental Ham Kabobs

Tip *Heat baby food right in the jar. Remove metal lid and warm on High for 15 to 20 seconds. Exact heating time varies according to size and temperature of jar, number of jars and amount of food in the jar.*

Oven-Baked Chicken

Juicy, tender chicken with minimum preparation.

1 (3-lb.) fryer, cut up
1 pkg. seasoned coating mix for chicken

Coat chicken with seasoned coating mix, according to directions on package. Place chicken in 7-1/2" x 12" utility dish, skin side down, with the meaty pieces to the outside of the dish. Cover with paper towel. Raise shelf. Cook on High for 10 minutes. Turn dish. Cook for 10 to 11 minutes more. Brown 6 minutes. Makes 4 servings.

Roast Chicken with Stuffing and Pan Gravy

The easiest Sunday dinner of all.

1 (4-lb.) roasting chicken
1 (6-1/2-oz.) pkg. stuffing mix
Salad oil

Pan Gravy:
1/2 cup pan drippings
1/4 cup flour

1-1/2 cups hot water or bouillon
Salt and pepper

Rinse chicken; pat dry. Prepare stuffing mix according to package directions. Stuff bird. Tie legs together; tuck wings under. Place, breast side down, on metal rack in 7-1/2" x 12" utility dish. Brush with oil. Cook on Medium for 10 minutes. Turn dish. Cook for a second 10 minutes. Turn breast side up and baste with drippings. Cook on Medium for a third 10 minutes. Turn dish. Cook for a final 10 minutes. Brown for 6 minutes. After browning, remove from dish, cover and let stand for 5 minutes. Serve with pan gravy. Makes 6 servings.

Pan Gravy:
Reserve 1/2 cup pan drippings. Stir in flour to make a smooth paste. Cook on High for 3 minutes, stirring twice. Add hot water or bouillon. Cook on High for 3 to 4 minutes or until thickened. Add salt and pepper to taste. Makes 2 cups.

Chicken Parmesan

Crisp on the outside—tender on the inside.

1 cut-up chicken
1/3 cup butter or margarine
1-1/2 cups Parmesan cheese

3 teaspoons paprika
2 teaspoons salt
1 teaspoon pepper

In 7-1/2" x 12" utility dish, melt butter or margarine on High for 40 seconds. Coat chicken with butter. Combine rest of the ingredients in a bag and add pieces of chicken one at a time. Shake to coat with crumb mixture. Place skin side down in the dish with the thickest pieces to the outer edge. Cover with paper towel to absorb any spatter. Cook on Medium, 10 minutes per pound. After half of the cooking time, turn chicken pieces over, skin side up. Sprinkle with remaining crumb mixture. Finish cooking on Medium. Brown as desired. Makes 4 servings.

Creamed Chicken

Delicious dinner for two—in a hurry.

1 pkg. frozen green peas with cream sauce
3/4 cup milk
1 tablespoon butter or margarine

Curry powder to taste
1 cup diced, cooked chicken

Put frozen peas, milk and butter or margarine in 2-quart casserole. Cover. Cook on High for 5 minutes. Remove from oven. Add the curry powder and stir until smooth. Fold in chicken. Cook on High for 1 to 2 minutes or until hot. Serve over rice. Makes 2 servings.

Deacon's Hot Curried-Chicken Salad

Popular demand will have you serving this often.

1 barbecued chicken, skinned and diced
1-1/4 cups chopped celery
1 small jar chopped pimientos
1 small green pepper, chopped
1 small onion, chopped
3 hard-cooked eggs, chopped
1/3 cup cashew nuts,
   coarsely chopped

1-1/4 cups mayonnaise
1/2 teaspoon salt
1/4 teaspoon pepper
1/4 teaspoon celery salt
Curry powder to taste
4 tablespoons lemon juice
1 cup chopped Cheddar cheese
1-1/2 cups crushed potato chips

In 7-1/2" x 12" utility dish, mix all the ingredients together, except the Cheddar cheese and potato chips. Raise shelf. Cook on High for 3 minutes. Stir. Cook for 2 minutes. Sprinkle with the Cheddar cheese. Cook for 1 minute. Sprinkle with potato chips. Brown 4 to 5 minutes. Makes 4 servings.

Chicken Marengo

Chicken in a tangy, colorful sauce.

2-1/2 lbs. chicken parts
1/4 cup flour
1/4 cup salad oil
1 (1-1/2-oz.) pkg. spaghetti-sauce mix

1/2 cup dry white wine
3 tomatoes, quartered
1/4 lb. fresh mushrooms, halved

Rinse chicken and pat dry. Coat with flour and roll in oil. Place skin side up in 7-1/2" x 12" utility dish, with the meaty pieces to the outside of the dish. Cover with wax paper. Cook on High for 8 minutes. Combine dry spaghetti-sauce mix, wine and tomatoes. Pour over chicken. Cover. Cook on High for 8 additional minutes. Add mushrooms. Cover. Cook on High for 1 minute. Makes 4 to 5 servings.

Chicken 'n Rice

A terrific meal in one casserole.

3 tablespoons butter or margarine
2 to 2-1/2 lbs. chicken parts
1/2 lb. brown-and-serve sausages,
   cut into chunks

1 (16-oz.) can stewed tomatoes
1 cup chicken bouillon
1/2 teaspoon salt
1 cup uncooked rice

In 4-quart casserole, melt butter or margarine on High for 35 seconds. Coat chicken parts with melted butter or margarine. Cover. Cook on High for 8 minutes. Combine remaining ingredients. Spoon over chicken. Cover. Cook on High for 15 minutes or until rice is cooked. Let stand, covered for 10 minutes before serving. Makes 4 to 5 servings.

Chicken in the Bag

Short cooking time shortened even more!

1 (2-1/2 to 3-lb.) frying chicken, cut up
1 (1-3/8-oz.) oven cooking bag with
   coating mix for chicken
1 (4-oz.) can mushrooms

Water
2 onions, quartered
1/2 cup catsup

Wash chicken; dry with paper towels. Place chicken in cooking bag, skin side up. Drain mushrooms; save liquid. Add water to make 1/2 cup. Arrange onions around chicken. Blend coating mix with the mushroom liquid and catsup. Pour sauce mixture over chicken. Close bag with rubber band or string. Place bag in 7-1/2" x 12" utility dish. Punch 4 small holes along top of bag. Cook on High for 10 minutes; turn dish. Cook for 10 minutes more. Add mushrooms and let stand for 10 minutes. Makes 4 to 5 servings.

Sherried Chicken Bake

Fast and fantastic. Try it plain or sauced.

2 full chicken breasts,
   (approximately 1-1/2 lbs.),
   skinned, boned, and halved lengthwise
1 cup cocktail sherry

1 small box dry coating mix for chicken
1 teaspoon thyme
1/2 teaspoon paprika
1/4 cup butter or margarine

Let chicken marinate in sherry for 3 minutes. In small bag, blend dry chicken coating mix with thyme and paprika. Coat chicken with mixture. In 7-1/2" x 12" utility dish, melt the butter or margarine on High for 40 seconds. Add chicken, coating both sides with melted butter or margarine. Place thick side of breast to the outer edge of the dish. Cover dish with plastic wrap. Cook on Medium for 7 minutes. Turn chicken over and rearrange in the dish. Cover dish with the plastic wrap. Cook 7 minutes more on Medium. Brown 6 to 8 minutes, if desired. Makes 4 servings.

Variation:
Serve on rice with Sherry-Mushroom Sauce.

Sherry-Mushroom Sauce:
1 (1-oz.) pkg. chicken-gravy mix
1/2 cup sliced fresh mushrooms
1 cup cocktail sherry that the chicken
   marinated in

1 cup dairy sour cream,
   room temperature

After chicken has cooked, remove from dish. Add chicken-gravy mix to the drippings. Stir well. Cook on High for 4 minutes. Add mushrooms and sherry. Cook on High for 2 minutes. Stir in sour cream. Heat on High for 1 minute. If desired, thin with additional sherry or water.

Chicken Dijon

A continental meal you can afford to serve often.

3 tablespoons butter or margarine
4 chicken breasts (about 2 lbs.), boned,
   skinned and halved lengthwise
2 tablespoons all-purpose flour

1 cup chicken broth
1/2 cup light cream
2 tablespoons Dijon-style mustard

In 7-1/2" x 12" utility dish, melt the butter or margarine on High for 35 seconds. Coat chicken on both sides with melted butter or margarine. Cover. Cook on High for 6 minutes. Turn dish. Cook on High for an additional 6 minutes. Place chicken on warm platter and set aside. Stir flour into drippings. Add broth and cream. Cook on High, stirring often, until mixture is thick. Stir in mustard. Pour sauce over chicken. Heat on High for 1-1/2 minutes. Makes 4 servings.

Chicken Breasts, French Style

Unbelievably delicious—worth the extra preparation time.

3 large chicken breasts (about 3 lbs.),
   boned, skinned and halved lengthwise
6 slices Prosciutto or thinly sliced ham
6 thin slices Swiss or American cheese
Pepper

2 tablespoons butter or margarine
1 (10-3/4-oz.) can cream-of-mushr[oom]
2 tablespoons dry white wine
1 (3-oz.) can sliced mushrooms,
   drained (optional)

Pound chicken breasts with wooden mallet until about 1/4-inch thick. Place 1 slice of ham and cheese on each. Tuck in sides and roll up as for jelly roll. Skewer with toothpick or tie securely. Sprinkle with pepper. Melt butter or margarine in 7-1/2" x 12" utility dish on High for 30 seconds. Coat chicken with melted butter or margarine. Cook on High for 10 minutes. Combine soup with wine and add mushrooms, if desired. Pour over chicken. Cover with wax paper. Cook on High for 10 to 11 minutes, turning dish once. Let stand 8 to 10 minutes before serving. Makes 6 servings.

Hawaiian Fried Chicken

Tender, moist chicken with subtle oriental flavor.

1/4 cup soy sauce
1/4 cup white wine
Juice of 1 lime
1 garlic clove, minced
1/4 teaspoon ground ginger

1/4 teaspoon oregano
1/4 teaspoon thyme
3 whole chicken breasts (about 3 lbs.), halved
1/4 cup flour
1/2 cup butter or margarine

Combine soy sauce with wine, lime juice, garlic, ginger, oregano and thyme. Pour over chicken. Marinate for several hours, turning 2 or 3 times. Drain sauce. Pat chicken dry with paper towels. Coat with flour. In 7-1/2" x 12" utility dish, melt butter or margarine on High for 1 minute. Add chicken, skin side down. Raise shelf. Cook on High for 9 to 10 minutes. Turn chicken; brush with butter. Cook on High for 9 to 10 minutes. Brown for 6 to 8 minutes. Makes 6 servings.

Country-Style Chicken

Everybody loves this fantastically simple combination.

1 (3-lb.) frying chicken, cut up
Seasoned flour

1/4 cup butter or margarine

Coat chicken with seasoned flour. Melt butter or margarine in 7-1/2" x 12" utility dish on High for 40 seconds. Roll chicken in melted butter or margarine. Place, skin side down, in utility dish with the meaty pieces to the outside. Cover with wax paper. Raise shelf. Cook on Medium for 15 minutes. Turn chicken over. Cook for 15 minutes more. Remove wax paper. Brown for 8 minutes. Let stand for 5 minutes. Makes 4 to 5 servings.

Chinese-Glazed Cornish Hen

You'll love the convenience of microwave defrosting.

2 Cornish hens, 15 to 18 oz. each
1 recipe Chinese Rice Stuffing

1 recipe Chinese Apricot Glaze
1/4 cup butter, melted

Thoroughly defrost Cornish hens as described in table, page 73. Remove giblets, rinse and dry. Stuff each hen with half of Chinese Rice Stuffing, close mouth of cavity securely with toothpicks. Tie legs of each hen together with string, then cover ends of legs with a small piece of foil (one piece of foil covering both legs). Place hens, breast side down, on wire rack in 7-1/2" x 12" utility dish. Brush with butter. Cook on Medium for 15 minutes. Turn hens breast side up. Brush with butter. Cook on Medium for 5 minutes. Brush a generous coating of Chinese Apricot Glaze on each hen. Continue to cook on Medium for 12 to 15 minutes, brushing twice with glaze until done. Let stand 10 minutes before serving. Makes 2 to 4 servings.

Chinese Rice Stuffing

Good stuffing for chicken, too.

1/4 cup butter
2 tablespoons minced onion
4 medium mushrooms, chopped
1/4 cup chopped dried apricots

1 tablespoon chopped dried parsley
1/8 teaspoon ginger
1-1/2 teaspoons soy sauce
1-1/2 cups cooked white or brown rice

In 1-quart casserole, combine butter, onion and mushrooms. Cover. Cook on High for 2 to 3 minutes or until vegetables are tender. Stir in remaining ingredients. Use to stuff 2 Cornish hens or 1 chicken. Makes about 1-3/4 cups of stuffing.

Chinese Apricot Glaze

Try this finishing touch on pork or chicken.

1/2 cup dried apricots
3/4 cup water
1-1/2 teaspoons grated orange peel
1/4 cup orange juice

3 tablespoons dark corn syrup
1 tablespoon cider vinegar
1 tablespoon soy sauce
1/2 teaspoon ground ginger

In 2-cup liquid measure, combine apricots and water. Cook on High for 3 to 4 minutes or until mixture boils. Turn to Low and continue cooking for 3 to 5 minutes or until apricots are soft and plump. Let stand a few minutes. Drain. Combine apricots and remaining ingredients in a blender container. Blend on low speed until smooth. Use to baste Cornish hens. Also good on chicken. Makes about 1-1/4 cups of glaze.

Chinese-Glazed Cornish Hen

Roast Turkey with Country Gravy

Don't wait for the holidays to try this.

1 (10-lb.) turkey
Salt
2 stalks celery, chopped
1 small onion, chopped
1/4 cup butter or margarine

1 (7-oz.) pkg. poultry dressing
3/4 cup water
1/2 cup oil
1/2 teaspoon brown sauce for gravy

Country Gravy:
1 cup pan drippings
1/2 cup flour

2 cups hot water, consommé or beef stock
Salt and pepper

Wash turkey; pat dry with paper towel. Sprinkle inside with salt. In 4-cup measure, combine celery and onion with butter or margarine. Cook on High for 5 minutes. Add to package dressing with water. Spoon into cavities of turkey. Tie legs together, then to tail. Close neck cavity with small wooden skewer. Tie string around center of turkey to hold wings against body. Combine oil and brown sauce for gravy. Brush bird with oil mixture. Place, breast side down, on metal rack in 7-1/2" x 12" utility dish. Place wax paper over bird. Allow 9-1/2 to 10-1/2 minutes per pound on Medium for total cooking time. Cook 1/4 of the total time, turn dish and baste with oil mixture. Cook 1/4 of the time, turn turkey, breast side up, and baste. Cook 1/4 of the time, turn dish again and baste. Cook the final 1/4 length of time. Remove from dish and cover with foil for 20 minutes. Serve with Country Gravy. Makes 8 servings.

Country Gravy:
Reserve 1 cup drippings in the utility dish. Stir in flour to make a smooth paste. Cook on High for 8 minutes, stirring twice. Add hot liquid and cook on High for 5 minutes more. Add salt and pepper to taste. Makes 3 cups.

Cranberry-Glazed Turkey Roast

The dynamic duo—turkey and cranberries.

1 (3-lb.) frozen, boneless, rolled turkey roast
1 (8-oz.) can whole-berry cranberry sauce
2 tablespoons orange marmalade

2 tablespoons red wine
1/4 teaspoon cinnamon
Melted butter or margarine

Thaw roast for 5 minutes per pound on Low. Let stand for 10 minutes halfway through thawing. Turn roast over halfway through thawing. In 4-cup measure, heat cranberry sauce, marmalade, wine and cinnamon on High for 2 minutes; set aside. Cut plastic bag from turkey, but do not remove net. Brush with melted butter or margarine. Place turkey on metal rack in 7-1/2" x 12" utility dish. Cover with wax paper. Cook on Medium for 11 minutes. Turn roast over and brush with cranberry glaze. Cook for a second 11 minutes. Turn dish and brush roast with glaze. Cook on Medium for a third 11 minutes. Remove wax paper. Brown 6 minutes. Remove roast from oven and cover with foil for 5 minutes. Serve with remaining sauce. Makes 6 servings.

Chicken Cordon Bleu

Keep this in your freezer for surprise company.

4 whole chicken breasts (about 4 lbs.)
   boned with all the skin possible intact
4 slices Prosciutto or Westphalian ham

4 thin slices Muenster or
   Monterey Jack cheese
2 tablespoons butter or margarine

Mushroom-Cheese Sauce:
2 tablespoons flour
Drippings from cooked chicken breasts
1 cup grated Cheddar or
   Monterey Jack cheese

1/4 cup milk
1/4 cup white wine
1/2 cup sliced fresh mushrooms
1/4 cup sliced green onion

Pound each breast to 1/4-inch thick. Place 1/2 slice of ham and cheese on each breast half. Be sure that cheese does not come near the edge of the chicken. Fold the sides together, pinning through the skin with round toothpicks. In 7-1/2" x 12" utility dish, melt 2 tablespoons butter or margarine on High for 30 seconds. Coat the chicken in the hot butter or margarine. Place the thick side of the breast towards the outside of the dish. Cover with wax paper. Raise shelf. Cook on Medium for 20 minutes. Turn chicken over, thick side towards the outside of the dish. Cover. Cook 20 minutes more on Medium. Uncover. Brown 5 to 6 minutes. Reserve drippings. Serve with Mushroom-Cheese Sauce. Makes 4 servings.

Sauce:
Stir flour into drippings and make a smooth paste. Add cheese and mix well. Add milk and wine and stir. Cook on High for 3 to 4 minutes or until mixture comes to medium boil. Add mushrooms. Cook on High for 1-1/2 to 2 minutes. Pour sauce over the Cordon Bleu. Garnish with green onions.

Mary's Chicken Divan

They'll never guess what gives it that tangy flavor.

2 (10-oz.) pkgs. frozen broccoli spears
2 whole chicken breasts (about 2 lbs.),
   boned, skinned and halved
2 (10-3/4-oz.) cans condensed cream-
   of-mushroom soup
1 cup mayonnaise

1 teaspoon lemon juice
1/2 teaspoon curry powder (optional)
1/2 cup shredded sharp Cheddar cheese
1/2 cup soft bread crumbs
2 tablespoons butter or margarine

Pierce packages and partially thaw the broccoli in the packages on High for 4-1/2 minutes. Place chicken in 7-1/2" x 12" utility dish. Cover with wax paper. Cook on High for 7 minutes. Remove chicken and slice. Arrange broccoli spears in the utility dish. Place sliced chicken over the broccoli. Combine soup, mayonnaise, lemon juice and curry powder, if desired. Pour over the chicken. Cover with plastic wrap. Raise shelf. Cook on High for 5 minutes. Remove plastic wrap and sprinkle the cheese on top of the casserole. Measure bread crumbs into a 1-cup measure and add butter or margarine. Heat on High for 1 minute. Mix well. Top casserole with bread crumbs. Brown for 4 minutes. Makes 4 servings.

Chicken-Noodle Casserole

Try this one again with tuna fish.

4 oz. noodles, cooked and drained
1 (10-3/4-oz.) can cream-of-mushroom soup
3/4 cup milk
1/4 lb. mild Cheddar cheese,
   grated (1 cup)
1/3 cup chopped green pepper

2 tablespoons chopped pimiento
1/2 teaspoon salt
1/4 teaspoon pepper
2 cups cooked, diced chicken
3/4 cup crushed potato chips

On cooktop, cook noodles according to package directions. Drain. Combine noodles with remaining ingredients, except potato chips, in a 2-1/2-quart casserole. Mix well. Cover. Cook on High for 10 minutes, stirring after half the cooking time. Stir. Sprinkle with potato chips. Brown 5 to 6 minutes or until top is browned as desired. Makes 6 servings.

Partially cook casserole, then stir, bringing center portion to the outer edges. After stirring, add topping and finish cooking.

Defrosting Uncooked Meats Table

Remove tape from freezer paper. Open ends of package. If meat is wrapped in foil, remove foil completely and wrap meat loosely in wax paper. Times are approximate and meat could take longer to defrost depending on temperature of freezer.

Cut	Procedure	Power Setting	Approximate Minutes Per Pound	Standing Time
BEEF				
Chuck or Pot Roast	Cover loosely with paper. Turn over halfway through defrosting time. Also see Freezer-to-Table Recipes, pages 52 and 53.	Low	4 to 5	10 minutes
Ground Beef	Cut in half halfway through defrosting time. Swing center cut to outside. Finish defrosting.	Low	5 to 6	5 to 10 minutes
Rib Roast or Rump Rost, boneless	Turn over halfway through defrosting time. Also see Freezer-to-Table Recipes, pages 52 and 53.	Low	5 to 6	10 minutes halfway, through defrosting time and at finish.
Round Steak Sirloin Steak	Cover loosely with paper. Halfway through defrosting time turn over or break apart if in pieces. Also see Freezer-to-Table Recipes, pages 52 and 53.	Low	4 to 5	10 minutes
VEAL				
Roast	Cover loosely with paper. Turn over halfway through defrosting time.	Low	4 to 5	10 minutes
Steak		Low	4 to 5	10 minutes
PORK				
Bacon	Cover loosely.	Low	2 to 3	
Chops	Cover loosely with paper. Turn over halfway through defrosting time and break apart if possible.	Low	4 to 5	10 minutes
Roast	Cover loosely with paper. Turn over halfway through defrosting time.	Low	5 to 6	10 minutes halfway through defrosting time
Spareribs	Cover loosely with paper. Turn over halfway through defrosting time and break apart.	Low	4 to 5	10 minutes
POULTRY				
Chicken, cut up	Cover loosely with paper. Turn over halfway through defrosting time and break pieces apart.	Low	5 to 6	10 minutes
Chicken, whole	Cover loosely with paper. Turn breast side down halfway through defrosting time.	Low	6 to 7	10 minutes halfway through defrosting time.
Cornish Game Hens	Cover loosely with paper. Turn over halfway through defrosting time. Rinse in cold water and dry.	Low	5 to 6	

Cut	Procedure	Power Setting	Approximate Minutes Per Pound	Standing Time
Turkey	Cover loosely with paper. Turn breast side down halfway through defrosting time.	Low	6 to 7	10 minutes halfway through defrosting time.
LAMB Roast	Cover loosely with paper. Turn over halfway through defrosting time.	Low	4 to 5	10 minutes halfway through defrosting time.
Steaks	Cover loosely with paper. Turn over halfway through defrosting time and break apart.	Low	4 to 5	10 minutes
OTHER MEATS Corned Beef	Leave in package. Turn over halfway through defrosting time.	Low	4 to 5	10 minutes
Hot Dogs, 1 2 5 or 6	Wrap in paper. Place between 2 paper plates.	Medium Medium Medium	1 1-3/4 to 2 3-1/2	
Liver, sliced	Turn over halfway through defrosting time. Let stand. Separate and rinse in cold water.	Low	4 to 5	10 minutes

Tender Beef Cooking Table

More about tender beef cooking, pages 40, 41.

CUT	Special Techniques	Internal Doneness	Power Setting	Approximate Minutes Per Pound	Browning and Standing Time
Ground Beef, Bulk	Place in utility dish or casserole. Stir and break apart during cooking. Looks a little pink, but color cooks out during standing time.	Well	High	3-1/2 to 5	Let stand 5 minutes.
Hamburger Patties	Shape 3 (1-inch thick) patties per pound. Place on metal rack in utility dish. Raise shelf to upper position. Turn patties over halfway through cooking time. Shows some pink spots until browned.	Medium	High	3 to 5	Brown 6 to 7 minutes with shelf remaining in upper position.
Meat Loaf	See Meat Loaf, page 48.				
Eye of Round Roast Watermelon Cut, Rump Roast	Insert garlic slivers; season. Place on metal rack in utility dish. Turn meat over halfway through cooking time. Shield ends with foil, if necessary.	Rare Medium Well Rare Medium Well	Medium Low	5 to 7 6 to 8 7 to 9 10 to 12 12 to 13 13 to 14	Brown or cover with foil. Use Stay Hot for 15 minutes.

Tender Beef Cooking Table (Continued)

CUT	Special Techniques	Internal Doneness	Power Setting	Approximate Minutes Per Pound	Browning and Standing Time
Liver	See Liver and Onions, page 51.	Medium Well	High	2-1/2 to 3-1/2	Let stand 3 minutes.
Rib Roasts, Standing, Bone-In	Season meat. Place in utility dish with cut side down for 1/3 of cooking time. Turn to other side for next 1/3. Drain fat. Stand on bones for last 1/3 of cooking time	Rare Medium Well	Medium	7 to 9 9 to 11 11 to 13	Brown and cover with foil. Use Stay Hot or let stand 10 minutes.
		Rare Medium Well	Low	10 to 13 13 to 15 15 to 16	
Small Roast Boned and Rolled First 4 Ribs Prime Rib	Season meat. Set on metal meat rack in utility dish. Cover with paper towels. Turn meat over halfway through cooking time. Drain fat.	Rare Medium Well	Medium	6 to 8 8 to 10 10 to 12	Remove paper towels. Brown and cover with foil. Use Stay Hot or let stand 10 to 15 minutes.
		Rare Medium Well	Low	8 to 10 10 to 12 12 to 14	
Large Roast. Boned and Rolled, 4th to 7th Ribs Prime Rib	Use same technique as recommended for small roast.	Rare Medium Well	Medium	8 to 10 10 to 12 13 to 14	Remove paper towels. Brown and cover with foil. Use Stay Hot or let stand 15 to 20 minutes.
		Rare Medium Well	Low	11 to 14 14 to 15 15 to 16	
Ribs, Beef Bones	Separate ribs. Put on metal rack in utility dish. Brush with sauce. Cover with wax paper. Place shelf in lower position. Drain halfway through cooking time.		High	4 to 5	Remove paper. Brown with shelf remaining in lower position until sauce is tacky.
Steaks, Bone-In, 1-inch thick	Season and place on metal rack in utility dish. Place shelf in upper position. Turn steak over halfway through cooking time.	Rare Medium Well	High	3 to 4 4-1/2 to 5 5 to 5-1/2	Brown with shelf remaining in upper position for 6 to 7 minutes.
Steaks, Boned, 1-inch thick	Use same technique as recommended for steaks, bone-in.	Rare Medium Well	High	2-1/2 to 3-1/2 3-1/2 to 4 4 to 4-1/2	Brown with shelf remaining in upper position for 8 to 10 minutes.
Steaks, Boned, Chateaubriand, 2-inches thick	Use same technique as recommended for steaks, bone-in.	Rare Medium Well	High	5 to 5-1/2 5-1/2 to 6-1/2 6-1/2 to 7-1/2	Brown with shelf remaining in upper position for 8 to 10 minutes.
Weiners, 1 lb.	Place on metal rack in utility dish or spoke-shape on platter. Cover with wax paper.		High	2-1/2 to 3-1/2	Remove wax paper and use Stay Hot for 10 minutes.
Weiner — 1	Wrap in wax paper		High	20 to 30 seconds	Remove wax paper and use Stay Hot for 10 minutes.

Tender Beef Cooking Table (Continued)

CUT	Special Techniques	Internal Doneness	Power Setting	Approximate Minutes Per Pound	Browning and Standing Time
Veal Rump Roast, Boned & Rolled	Insert garlic slivers; season lightly. Put in roasting bag or cover with wax paper. Turn meat over halfway through cooking time.		Low	14 to 16	Remove bag or wax paper. Brown and cover with foil. Use Stay Hot or let stand 10 to 15 minutes.
Veal Steaks, Bone-In 1-inch thick	Place meat on metal rack in utility dish. Raise shelf to upper position. Turn steaks over halfway through cooking time.		Medium	7 to 9	Brown 5 minutes.

These cooking times are for foods taken directly from the refrigerator. If the food is at room temperature, reduce cooking time slightly and check doneness.

Less-Tender Beef Cooking Table

More about less-tender-beef cooking, pages 41, 42.

Cut	Special Techniques	Power Setting	Approximate Minutes Per Pound	Browning and Standing Time
Chuck Roast, 2-inches thick	Season and put in oven bag or covered casserole. Do not add liquid. Turn dish each quarter of cooking time.	Low	14 to 16	Leave covered and let stand 10 to 15 minutes.
Corned Beef	Put in oven bag. Do not add liquid. Make knife slits in bag. Turn dish each quarter of cooking time.	Low	18 to 20	Leave covered and let stand 20 minutes.
Flank Steak, Rolled	See Stuffed Flank Steak, page 44.	Low	18 to 20	Leave covered and let stand 10 minutes.
Round Steak, Pieces or Cubes	Coat cubes in oil. Cook uncovered 3 to 4 minutes on High. Add 1/2 cup warm water per pound. Cover. Cook remaining time on Low.	Low	18 to 20	Leave covered and let stand 10 minutes.
Rump Roast, Boned & Rolled, 5-inch diameter	Insert garlic slivers. Place in oven bag or covered casserole with fresh onions. Make knife slits in bag. Turn dish once.	Low	11 to 13	Leave covered and let stand 15 minutes.

These cooking times are for foods taken directly from the refrigerator. If the food is at room temperature, reduce cooking time slightly and check doneness.

Pork Cooking Table

More about pork cooking, page 42.

Cut	Special Techniques	Power Setting	Approximate Minutes Per Pound	Browning and Standing Time
Loin, Boned and Rolled	Rub in seasoning. Place fat side down on rack. Cover with wax paper. Turn over halfway through cooking time. Shield ends, if shape requires.	Low	12 to 14	Remove wax paper and brown. Cover with foil and use Stay Hot or let stand 15 minutes.
Loin, Bone-In	Same as above.	Low	13 to 15	Same as above.
Shoulder, Boned and Rolled	Insert garlic slivers and season. Place on metal rack in utility dish. Cover with wax paper. Turn over halfway through cooking time. Shield ends, if shape requires.	Low	12 to 14	Remove wax paper and brown. Cover with foil and use Stay Hot or let stand 15 minutes.
Tenderloin, Boned	Cut in half crosswise. Season or brush with a sauce. Place on metal rack in utility dish. Cover with wax paper. Turn over halfway through cooking time.	Medium	6 to 7	Remove wax paper and brown. Use Stay Hot for total of 15 minutes.
Steaks or Chops, 1/2-inch thick	Rub with liquid smoke and sprinkle with garlic salt. Place tenderloin side toward center of dish. Cover with wax paper. Turn dish once.	Medium	4-1/2 to 5-1/2	Remove wax paper and brown, or let stand for 8 to 10 minutes.
1-inch thick	Same as above.	Medium	6-1/2 to 7-1/2	Same as above.
Ribs, Country-Style	Separate ribs into single bones. Place in utility dish with bone side toward center. Cover with wax paper. Drain fat halfway through cooking time. Brush with sauce, replace wax paper and turn dish.	High	6-1/2 to 7-1/2	Remove wax paper and drain fat. Brown or let stand for 8 to 10 minutes.
Spareribs	Separate ribs into single bones. Stand on side in utility dish. Cover with plastic wrap (because of large amount of bone). Drain fat halfway through cooking time, brush with sauce, cover with plastic wrap and turn dish.	High	14 to 16	Remove plastic wrap. Place shelf in lower position. Brown 8 to 10 minutes.
Weiners, 1 lb.	Place on metal rack in utility dish or in a spoke-shape on a platter. Cover with wax paper.	High	2-1/2 to 3-1/2	Remove wax paper. Use Stay Hot for 10 minutes.
Sausage, Bulk or Links	Place on metal rack in utility dish. Cover with wax paper. Turn over halfway through cooking time.	Medium	4-1/2 to 5-1/2	Remove wax paper and brown.

These cooking times are for foods taken directly from the refrigerator. If the food is at room temperature, reduce cooking time slightly and check doneness.

Ham Cooking Table

More about ham cooking, page 42.

Cut	Special Techniques	Power Setting	Approximate Minutes Per Pound	Browning and Standing Time
Canned, Boneless	Use foil to cover small end for first half of cooking time. Lay wax paper over top and turn meat over halfway through cooking time.	Medium	10 to 13	Remove wax paper and brown. Cover with foil and use Stay Hot, or let stand 15 minutes.
Shank or Butt End, Bone-In	Start with cut side up. Cover with wax paper. Turn ham cut side down halfway through cooking.	Medium	8 to 10	Remove wax paper and brown. Cover with foil and use Stay Hot, or let stand 15 minutes.
Tavern, Boneless	Lay wax paper over top. Turn meat over halfway through cooking. Turn dish at each quarter of cooking time.	Medium	6 to 7	Remove wax paper and brown. Cover with foil and use Stay Hot, or let stand 15 minutes.
Steak, 1-inch thick	Cover with wax paper. Place shelf in upper position. Turn over halfway through cooking time.	Medium	4-1/2 to 5-1/2	Remove wax paper and brown. Let stand with Stay Hot 15 minutes.
Bacon	Substitute paper tray and pleated paper towels for metal rack in utility dish, if you choose. Cover with paper towel to prevent grease spatters.	High	about 1 minute per slice	Remove paper towel and use Stay Hot.

These cooking times are for foods taken directly from the refrigerator. If the food is at room temperature, reduce cooking time slightly and check doneness.

Lamb Roasting Table

More about lamb cooking, page 41.

Cut	Special Techniques	Internal Doneness	Power Setting	Approximate Minutes Per Pound	Browning and Standing Time
Leg, Boned and Rolled	Rub in garlic powder. Give dish a half-turn and turn meat over halfway through cooking time.	Medium Well / Medium Well	Medium / Low	9 to 11 / 11 to 13 / 11 to 13 / 13 to 15	Brown 7 to 8 minutes and use Stay Hot 10 to 15 minutes, or let stand.
Leg, Bone-In	Shield shank end with foil. Remove foil after half the cooking time. Give dish a half-turn and turn meat over halfway through cooking time.	Medium Well / Medium Well	Medium / Low	10 to 12 / 12 to 14 / 13 to 15 / 15 to 16	Brown 7 to 8 minutes and use Stay Hot 10 to 15 minutes, or let stand.
Loin, or Rack Bone-In	Shield ends of bone with foil. Remove foil after half the cooking time. Rub with seasonings. Give dish a half-turn halfway through cooking time.	Medium	High	6-1/2 to 7-1/2	Brown 7 to 8 minutes and use Stay Hot 10 to 15 minutes, or let stand.
Steaks or Chops, Bone-In, 1-inch thick	Rub with seasonings. Put on metal rack in utility dish with bone toward center of dish. Place shelf in upper position. Turn chops over halfway through cooking time.	Medium	High	3-1/2 to 4-1/2	Brown 7 minutes.
Pieces or Chunks Cut into 1-inch Cubes	Coat cubes with oil and lightly season. Place shelf in upper position. Stir twice during cooking.	Medium	High	4 to 5	Brown 5 minutes or let stand.

These cooking times are for foods taken directly from the refrigerator. If the food is at room temperature, reduce cooking time slightly and check doneness.

Poultry Roasting Table

More about poultry cooking, page 43.

Type	Special Techniques	Power Setting	Approximate Minutes Per Pound	Browning and Standing Time
Chicken Fryer, Whole	Place fryer on its side, wing down, on meat rack. Cook 1/3 of time and turn over. Cook next 1/3 of time. Turn breast up for last 1/3 of cooking time.	High / Medium	6-1/2 to 7-1/2 / 9 to 11	Brown 8 to 10 minutes or use Stay Hot, uncovered.
Chicken Fryer, Pieces	Place in utility dish with the thickest parts facing the outer edge and the smaller, less meaty pieces placed in center.	High / Medium	6-1/2 to 7-1/2 / 9 to 11	Brown 8 to 10 minutes or use Stay Hot, uncovered.

Poultry Roasting Table (Continued)

Type	Special Techniques	Power Setting	Approximate Minutes Per Pound	Browning and Standing Time
Chicken Fryer, All White Meat	Place in utility dish with thickest part facing the outer edge.	High Medium	5-1/2 to 6-1/2 8 to 10	Brown 6 to 8 minutes or use Stay Hot, uncovered.
Cornish Game Hen	Have butcher saw in half lengthwise while still frozen. Thaw before cooking. Place breast side down for 1/2 of cooking time; finish with breast up.	High Medium	5-1/2 to 7-1/2 9 to 11	Place shelf in upper position and brown 5 minutes on Stay Hot, uncovered. Let stand 5 minutes covered with foil.
Duck, Geese, Pheasant	Covered with wax paper or paper shopping bag. DO NOT USE A RECYCLED PAPER BAG. Cook 1/3 of cooking time on its side, wing down. Prick skin. Turn over with other wing down for next 1/3 of cooking time. Siphon fat, replace paper and turn breast up for last 1/3 of cooking time.	Medium	10 to 11	Remove paper cover and brown 8 to 10 minutes or use Stay Hot, uncovered.
Turkey, Whole	See Roast Turkey With Country Gravy, page 70. Or rub with oil or unsalted butter. Place breast down inside paper shopping bag. DO NOT USE A RECYCLED PAPER BAG. Cook 1/4 of total cooking time and turn dish. Cook 1/4 more of cooking time and turn breast up. Cook 1/4 more of cooking time and turn dish. Finish cooking.	Medium	9 to 11	Remove bag. Use Stay Hot or let stand 20 minutes covered with foil.
Turkey, Boned and Rolled	See Cranberry-Glazed Turkey Roast, page 70. Thaw before cooking. Cover with wax paper. Turn dish halfway through cooking time.	Medium	8-1/2 to 9-1/2	Uncover and brown to crisp skin, or let stand 10 minutes covered with foil.
Turkey, Bone-In, Half Breast	Shield thin edges with foil. Remove foil halfway through cooking time. Cover with wax paper. Turn at each 1/4 of cooking time.	Medium	9 to 11	Uncover. Brown 8 to 10 minutes. Let stand 5 minutes more covered with foil.
Turkey, Ground Patties	Place on metal meat rack in utility dish. Place shelf in upper position. Cook 1/2 of cooking time. Turn over.	High	3 to 4	Brown 5 minutes.

These cooking times are for foods taken directly from the refrigerator. If the food is at room temperature, reduce cooking time slightly and check doneness.

Fish & Seafood

Fish cooked by microwave tastes better than fish cooked by any other method. The texture is moist and tender and the flavor is delectable. Most fish is versatile. It can be barbecued, curried, or served with a sauce. An especially elegant dish is Lobster Thermidor. Equally delicious but more economical is Tuna Tetrazzini. Use the Seafood Table on page 89 to cook fish more simply, then dress it up with a sauce from the Sauce section of this book. Try rich Béchamel Sauce or pungent Creole Sauce.

Preparation—Rinse fish and pat dry. Cook with or without butter, margarine or oil. Season the fish and cook according to the Seafood Table. Coat fish with bread or cracker crumbs, corn meal or brush with a sauce, according to the recipe used. Always defrost fish before cooking with microwaves. Otherwise the center retains ice crystals even though the edges are cooked. To prevent the edges from cooking faster than the center, place the thicker edge of a fillet toward the outside of the cooking dish or overlap thin fillet edges to make the thickness more uniform. You can also roll a fillet to compensate for uneven thickness.

Utensil—Use a utility dish, platter or casserole with a lid. Select one that best fits the shape and quantity of fish. Plastic wrap or wax paper can be used for a lid. Use paper towels to cover the cooking dish if the fish is breaded. This prevents the breading from getting moist and from popping out of the dish. Cleaned sea shells make good cooking and serving dishes. The shells don't absorb microwaves and don't affect cooking time.

Length of Cooking—Fish is a naturally tender food, so requires little cooking. Most fish is cooked on High, but scallops and snails are exceptions and are cooked on Medium. Timing will vary slightly according to the thickness and amount. For example, if fish is less than 1/2-inch thick, use 1/2 to 1 minute-per-pound less than the time given on the table. Doubling the amount of fish requires about 50% more cooking time. One pound may cook in 5 minutes, but 2 pounds cook in 7-1/2 minutes. Fresh fish may cook a minute or so faster than frozen fish which has been thawed.

Test for Doneness—Fish requires little standing time. Because it cooks quickly, cooking should start only when the rest of the meal is nearly ready. Check doneness with a fork—fish should flake or fall apart easily. Overcooking results in dry, tough fish.

See Fish and Seafood Cooking Table, page 89.

81

Lobster Thermidor

A delicacy in rich sauce.

1/3 cup butter
1/2 cup sifted flour
3 cups half and half, room temperature
2 tablespoons white wine
1/4 teaspoon dry mustard
Pinch of cayenne pepper

1/4 cup butter
1/2 lb. fresh mushrooms, sliced
3 cups cooked lobster meat, cut in 1-inch pieces
1/4 cup grated Parmesan cheese
1-1/2 teaspoons salt
Parmesan cheese

In 4-quart casserole, melt 1/3 cup butter on High in 40 seconds. Stir in flour to make a paste. Add half and half gradually. Cook sauce on Medium for 13 minutes, stirring occasionally. Add wine, mustard and cayenne to sauce and set aside. Melt 1/4 cup butter in a 2-quart casserole on High for 40 seconds. Add mushrooms and sauté on High for 4 minutes. Add mushroom mixture to sauce along with lobster, 1/4 cup cheese and salt. Heat on High for 5 minutes. Sprinkle Parmesan cheese over top. Brown for 5 minutes. Serve over cooked rice. Makes 4 servings.

Seafood Newburg

A most impressive dish.

2 tablespoons butter or margarine
2 tablespoons flour
1-1/2 cups light cream
2 tablespoons dry white wine
1 cup sliced fresh mushrooms
1/2 teaspoon salt
1/8 teaspoon onion salt

1/8 teaspoon pepper
Dash nutmeg
2 egg yolks
1 cup cooked lobster tails, cut into small chunks
1 cup cooked crab meat or shrimp
Chopped chives

In 2-quart casserole, melt butter or margarine on High for 30 seconds. Stir in flour to make a smooth paste. Add cream, wine, mushrooms and seasonings. Cook on High for 5 to 6 minutes, stirring often. Beat egg yolks. Stir part of sauce into yolks. Then return egg-yolk mixture to casserole. Cook on Medium for 2 minutes, stirring every 15 seconds. Stir in seafood. Cook on High for 1 minute or until hot. Sprinkle with chives. Serve in baked patty shells or toast cups. Makes 4 to 5 servings.

Tip *To separate cold bacon slices easily, warm in the package on High for 15 to 20 seconds. Let stand 3 to 5 minutes.*

Salmon Newburg

Delectable sauce glamorizes an old favorite.

1/2 cup Basic Creamy-Sauce Mix, page 128
1 cup light cream
1/2 cup water
3 egg yolks, slightly beaten
3 tablespoons dry white wine
2 teaspoons lemon juice

1/4 teaspoon salt
1/4 teaspoon dried tarragon, crushed
1 (16-oz.) can salmon, drained and bones removed, broken into chunks
4 frozen patty shells, baked

In 2-quart casserole, combine sauce mix, cream and water. Cook on High for 2 minutes until thickened and bubbly, stirring often. Stir small amount of hot mixture into egg yolks. Return egg-yolk mixture to casserole. Cook on High for about 1 minute or until thick, stirring often. Stir in wine, lemon juice, salt and tarragon. Add salmon chunks. Cook on High for 2 minutes or until hot. Spoon into baked patty shells. Makes 4 servings.

Scalloped Oysters

Try this gourmet favorite in your microwave.

1/2 cup butter
2 cups coarse cracker crumbs (40 saltine crackers)
1/2 teaspoon salt
1/8 teaspoon pepper
1/2 teaspoon Worcestershire sauce

1/4 cup minced celery
1 pint oysters, drained; reserve liquor
1/4 cup (approximately) oyster liquor, plus milk to equal 3/4 cup
Minced parsley

Melt butter on High for 45 seconds. Combine with cracker crumbs, salt, pepper, Worcestershire sauce and celery. Spread 1/3 of mixture in a 2-quart buttered casserole. Layer 1/2 oysters over crumb mixture. Repeat layers, leaving top with leftover crumb mixture. Pour oyster liquor and milk mixture over contents of dish. Cook on High for 15 minutes, rotating 1/4 turn halfway through cooking time. Let stand 5 minutes. Garnish with parsley. Makes 6 servings.

Tip *To soften butter or margarine, open wrapper and heat on High for 5 seconds. Let stand 30 seconds and repeat until the desired softness is reached.*

Poached Salmon Steaks

A delicious favorite with tasty sauce.

1-1/2 cups hot water
1/3 cup dry white wine
2 peppercorns
1 lemon, thinly sliced

1 bay leaf
1 tablespoon instant minced onion
1 teaspoon seasoned salt
4 or 5 salmon steaks

Sauce:
1/2 cup dairy sour cream
1 tablespoon minced parsley

1 teaspoon lemon juice
1/2 teaspoon dried dill weed

In 7-1/2" x 12" utility dish, combine all ingredients except salmon and heat on High for 5 minutes or until boiling. Carefully place fish in hot liquid. Cover with plastic wrap. Cook on High for 2 minutes. Let stand 5 minutes. Drain. Serve with sauce. Makes 4 to 5 servings.

Sauce:
Combine sauce ingredients. Serve with salmon.

Tuna Patties

Enhance tuna with vegetable sauce.

2 eggs, slightly beaten
1 cup soft bread crumbs
1 tablespoon pickle relish
2 teaspoons instant minced onion
2 teaspoons lemon juice
1/2 teaspoon Worcestershire sauce

2 (6-1/2-oz.) cans tuna, drained and flaked
2 tablespoons butter or margarine
1 (8-oz.) pkg. frozen peas with cream sauce
Milk
Butter
2 hard-cooked eggs

In bowl, combine eggs with bread crumbs, relish, onion, lemon juice and Worcestershire sauce. Add tuna; mix thoroughly. Shape into 4 patties about 1-inch thick. Raise shelf. In 7-1/2" x 12" utility dish, melt butter on High for 30 seconds. Arrange patties in dish with butter. Cover with wax paper. Cook on High for 3 minutes. Turn patties over. Cover. Cook 2 minutes more on High. Uncover and brown 5 minutes. Put frozen peas in a 4-cup measure and combine with amount of milk and butter as indicated on package of peas. Cook on High for 4 minutes, stirring once. Peel and chop eggs; add to sauce. Pour over cooked tuna patties. Makes 4 servings.

Poached Salmon Steaks

Tip Crisp a plateful of stale crackers or chips on High for 45 seconds to 1 minute.

Tuna Tetrazzini

A new idea for a family favorite.

1/4 cup butter or margarine
1/4 cup flour
1 cup light cream
1 cup chicken bouillon
2 tablespoons white wine
1/2 teaspoon seasoned salt

1/2 cup grated Cheddar cheese
1/4 cup sliced green onions
1 (2-oz.) can sliced mushrooms, drained
2 (6-1/2-oz.) can tuna, drained
2 cups cooked thin spaghetti
1/4 cup fresh-chopped parsley

In 7-1/2" x 12" utility dish, melt butter or margarine on High for 40 seconds. Stir in flour, then cream, bouillon, wine and seasoned salt. Cook on High for 5 minutes, stirring twice. Fold in Cheddar cheese, green onions, mushrooms, tuna and drained spaghetti. Cover with wax paper. Cook on High for 3 to 4 minutes. Garnish with chopped parsley. Makes 4 to 5 servings.

Shrimp Curry

An exotic dish for an elegant dinner.

1 cup diced celery
1/2 cup chopped onion
1/4 cup butter
5 tablespoons flour
1 teaspoon salt
1 teaspoon curry powder
1/2 teaspoon sugar

1/8 teaspoon ginger
2 chicken-bouillon cubes
2 cups hot water
1 lb. cooked shrimp, drained
1/2 teaspoon lemon juice
2 tablespoons sherry

In 1-1/2-quart casserole, combine celery, onion, and butter. Cover. Cook on High for 6 to 7 minutes, until onions and celery are limp. Stir in flour, salt, curry powder, sugar and ginger. Cover. Cook on High for 1 minute. Dissolve bouillon cubes in water. Gradually add bouillon to flour mixture, stirring until smooth. Cover. Cook on High for 5 to 7 minutes until thickened and smooth, stirring occasionally. Add shrimp and lemon juice. Cover. Heat on High for 2 to 3 minutes to heat shrimp. Stir in sherry. Serve over hot rice with condiments. Makes 4 to 6 servings.

Condiments:
Chopped peanuts, coconut, chopped hard-cooked egg, crisp crumbled bacon, chutney, raisins.

Shrimp Curry

Tip *When estimating total meat-preparation time, remember to allow for 10 to 15 minutes standing time after meat is removed from the oven.*

Barbecued Halibut Steaks

So good you'll think you're at a seashore barbecue.

4 halibut steaks (about 2-lbs.), 1-inch thick
1/4 cup catsup
2 tablespoons salad oil
2 tablespoons lemon juice

1 teaspoon Worcestershire sauce
1/2 teaspoon prepared mustard
1/4 teaspoon garlic salt
Several drops liquid smoke

Arrange halibut steaks in 7-1/2" x 12" utility dish or serving platter. Combine remaining ingredients. Brush fish with sauce and cover with wax paper. Raise shelf. Cook on High for 3 minutes. Brush with sauce. Cook another 3 to 5 minutes. Brown 5 minutes. Makes 4 servings.

Fillets Amandine

Seafarer's delight.

1/4 cup slivered, blanched almonds
2 tablespoons butter or margarine
3 tablespoons butter or margarine
2 tablespoons lemon juice

1-1/2 lbs. fish fillets, cut into
    individual portions
1/2 teaspoon salt

In 2-cup measure, combine almonds and 2 tablespoons butter or margarine. Cook on High 2 to 3 minutes or until golden brown. In 7-1/2" x 12" utility dish, melt 3 tablespoons butter or margarine on High for 35 seconds. Stir in lemon juice and add fish. Cover with wax paper. Cook on High for 2 minutes. Turn dish and cook 3 minutes (depending on thickness of fillets). Sprinkle with salt and buttered almonds. Makes 2 servings.

Sole Veronique

An intriguing combination of tastes and textures.

1 lb. fillet of sole
1 cup sauterne wine
1/4 cup butter or margarine
1 tablespoon cornstarch

2/3 cup light cream
1/2 teaspoon salt
1 cup seedless grapes

Cut fish into serving-size portions. In 7-1/2" x 12" utility dish, pour 2/3 cups wine over fish. Reserve 1/3 cup wine. Cover with plastic wrap. Cook on High 4 to 5 minutes, turning dish once. Drain fillets. In 4-cup measure, melt butter or margarine on High for 40 seconds. Dissolve cornstarch in cream. Add salt and stir into melted butter or margarine. Add 1/3 cup reserved wine to cream mixture. Cook on High for 1 minute, stirring once. Cook on Medium for 2 to 2-1/2 minutes, stirring every 30 seconds to prevent sauce from curdling. Add grapes. Place cooked sole in platter suitable for use in microwave (page 9). Pour sauce with grapes over fish. Cook on High for 30 seconds. Makes 3 to 4 servings.

Lemon-Butter-Drenched Scampi

Tender meat from the sea drenched in elegant golden sauce.

1 lb. large, raw shrimp
1/4 cup butter or margarine
1 garlic clove, minced
2 tablespoons lemon juice

1 tablespoon minced parsley
1/2 teaspoon salt
1/8 teaspoon pepper

Peel shrimp, clean and remove vein. Split along back curve, cutting deep, almost to edge. Open, then press flat, butterfly-style. In 7-1/2" x 12" utility dish, melt butter or margarine on High for 40 seconds. Add the remaining ingredients. Stir well to coat shrimp. Cook on High for 1 minute. Stir. Cook another 1-1/2 to 2 minutes. Serve immediately. Makes 2 servings.

Fish & Seafood Cooking Table

Shellfish and Fish	Special Techniques	Power Setting	Approximate Minutes Per Pound	Standing Time or Stay Hot Time
Fish Fillets, 1/2-inch thick Salmon, Halibut, Cod, Swordfish, Red Snapper or Local Varieties.	Dry fish on paper towel. Melt butter in utility dish. Bread if desired. Coat both sides with butter; sprinkle with blend of seasonings. Cover with wax paper tucked beneath ends of dish.	High	4-1/2 to 5-1/2. Thicker fillets require slightly longer cooking.	Cooked when flakes; serve immediately. If breaded, raise shelf. Remove paper and brown. Use Stay Hot to hold crisp.
Fish Steaks, 1-inch thick Salmon, Halibut, Cod, Swordfish or Local Varieties.	Dry fish on paper towels. Melt butter in utility dish; coat both sides fish steak. Sprinkle blend of seasoning or lemon juice on top. Cover with wax paper. Salt after cooking.	High	5 to 6	Cooked when flakes, serve immediately.
Whole Fish Trout, Catfish or Local Varieties.	Dry fish and season as you like. No extra timing needed if stuffed. Cover with wax paper.	High	4 to 6	Let stand 5 minutes.
Lobster Tails	Have butcher split shell in half, but not thru underside, leaving joined also at tail. Cook meat side up. Brush with melted butter, season.	High	1 (8-oz.) tail — 2 to 3 minutes 2 (8-oz.) tails — 5 to 6 minutes	Cover with wax paper and let stand 5 minutes.
Shrimp, Green	Peel; clean and remove vein. Brush with melted butter; sprinkle with seasoning. Arrange 1/2 lb. like starburst on 9-inch pie plate. Or cook 1 lb. around edge of utility dish. Cook covered, turning dish once.	High	2 to 3	Cooked when meat loses its translucency. Serve immediately.
Shrimp, Cooked	Reheating is all that is needed. Can be added to a cooked sauce.	High	3 to 5	Let stand if it is in a sauce.

Fish & Seafood Cooking Table (Continued)

Shellfish and Fish	Special Techniques	Power Setting	Approximate Minutes Per Pound	Standing Time or Stay Hot Time

Crab, Cooked
  Stone
  Snow crab
  Dungeness (or other)
  King Crab
	Reheating is all that is needed. Stir halfway through cooking time. Can be added to a cooked sauce.	High	3 to 5	Let stand 3 to 5 minutes if in a casserole. Serve immediately if just reheated.

Squid*	Clean squid; cut mantle in half lengthwise. In a casserole, add 1 cup boiling water to single layer of squid. Cover. Turn dish halfway through cooking time.	High	9 to 11	Let stand, covered, 10 minutes. Drain and chill.
Scallops	Dry on paper towel. Melt butter in utility dish. Stir in scallops. Arrange larger around edge and smaller in center. Cover with wax paper.	Medium	7 to 8	Remove from dish and serve immediately.
Clams, Fresh* 24 Clams	In 8-1/2 x 13 x 2 utility dish, bring 1 cup water to boil on High for 3 minutes. Arrange clams evenly in bottom of dish. Cover with plastic wrap.	High	7 to 9 minutes	Let stand until clams open.
12 Clams	In 8-inch dish, bring 1/2 cup water to boil on High for 1-1/2 minutes. Arrange clams evenly in bottom of dish. Cover with plastic wrap.	High	3 to 5 minutes	Let stand until clams open.
Oysters, 6 live, fresh*	In 2-quart casserole, melt 1 tablespoon butter with 1/4 cup water; bring to boil on High for 1 minute. Arrange oysters evenly. Add 1/4 cup dry white wine and 2 medium garlic cloves, finely chopped. Cover; cook. Reserve liquid.	High	3 to 4 minutes	Let stand, covered, 2 to 3 minutes until shells open slightly. Open and serve on half shell. Use liquid for dipping.

These cooking times are for foods taken directly from the refrigerator. If the food is at room temperature, reduce cooking time slightly and check doneness.

*Information courtesy of National Marine Fisheries

TO DEFROST SEAFOOD:
Rewrap loosely in wax paper. Defrost on Low for 4 minutes per pound. Let stand 5 to 10 minutes to finish the thawing process.

Tip

To rehydrate dried fruits, cover with water or other liquid. Heat on High for 5 to 6 minutes. Let stand 5 minutes.

One-Dish Meals

Every family has favorite one-dish meals, usually with international flavors. You can serve them often, and explore new recipes, using the speed and convenience of your microwave oven.

Beef Enchiladas with Cheese are satisfying flavors from Mexico and the Southwest. Spaghetti with Meat Sauce is standard fare everywhere, but have you tried Lasagne International? Mandarin-Style Steak and Swedish Cabbage-Rolls give you flavors from far corners of the world.

Traditional favorites include New England Meat Pie and Corned Beef and Cabbage, both so much easier in your microwave. Good nutrition and memories of fine food will result from these delicious one-dish meals.

Lasagne International

Spicy sausage is the special ingredient.

1 lb. Italian sausage, casings removed
1 (16-oz.) can tomatoes, cut up
1 (6-oz.) can tomato paste
1/4 teaspoon dried basil, crushed
1/8 teaspoon garlic salt
16 oz. ricotta or cottage cheese
1/4 cup grated Parmesan cheese

1 tablespoon chopped parsley
1 egg, slightly beaten
1/2 teaspoon salt
1/8 teaspoon pepper
1 (8-oz.) pkg. cooked lasagne noodles
8 oz. mozzarella cheese, sliced

In 4-quart casserole, break up sausage and cook on High for 3 minutes, stirring once. Drain excess fat. Add tomatoes, tomato paste, basil and garlic salt. Cook, uncovered, on High for 10 minutes, stirring twice. In mixing bowl, stir together ricotta or cottage cheese, Parmesan cheese, parsley, egg, salt and pepper. Spoon a little meat sauce into bottom of 7-1/2" x 12" utility dish. Arrange half the cooked noodles over sauce, then half the ricotta or cottage-cheese mixture, half the mozzarella cheese and half the meat sauce. Repeat. Cover with plastic wrap. Cook on High for 4 minutes. Turn dish. Cook 4 to 6 minutes or until hot. Let stand 10 minutes. Makes 6 to 7 servings.

Mock Lasagne

The homemade meat sauce is in your freezer.

1 qt. Basic Meat Sauce, page 50
1/2 teaspoon dried oregano leaves, crushed
1/4 teaspoon dried thyme leaves, crushed
1/4 lb. Monterey Jack cheese, thinly sliced

1 cup cottage cheese
6 oz. medium noodles, cooked and drained
1/4 cup grated Parmesan cheese

Combine meat sauce with oregano and thyme. Spread 1/3 of the meat sauce in bottom of 7-1/2" x 12" utility dish. Add in layers half the Jack cheese, half the cottage cheese and half the noodles. Repeat, using 1/3 more of the meat sauce, the remaining Jack cheese, cottage cheese and noodles. Spread with remaining meat sauce. Sprinkle with Parmesan cheese. Cover with wax paper. Cook on High for 4 minutes. Turn dish. Cook another 4 minutes. Let stand several minutes before serving. Makes 6 servings.

Spaghetti with Meat Sauce

So easy your youngsters can put it together.

1 lb. lean ground beef
1 medium onion, chopped
1 garlic clove, minced
1 (28-oz.) can tomatoes, cut up
1/2 cup chopped celery
1/2 cup water
1/4 cup Burgundy wine
1 (6-oz.) can tomato paste

2 tablespoons chopped parsley
1 tablespoon brown sugar
1 teaspoon dried oregano leaves, crushed
1 teaspoon salt
1/4 teaspoon dried thyme leaves, crushed
1 bay leaf
3 cups cooked spaghetti
Parmesan cheese

In 4-quart casserole, crumble beef. Add onion. Cook on High for 4 minutes, stirring twice. Add remaining ingredients except spaghetti and cheese. Cover. Cook on High for 5 minutes. Stir. Cook 10 minutes, stirring once. Serve sauce over spaghetti. Sprinkle with cheese. Makes 4 to 5 servings.

Variation:
Place ingredients from garlic through brown sugar in blender and puree. Add this pureed sauce and remaining seasonings to meat mixture. Continue to follow recipe.

Tip *To soften 1 cup of hard brown sugar, add a slice of white bread or an apple wedge and heat, covered, on High for 30 to 45 seconds.*

Beef and Cheese Bake

A healthful protein-packed dish.

1 lb. ground beef
2 (8-oz.) cans tomato sauce
Salt and pepper
1/4 cup chopped green onions
2 tablespoons chopped green pepper

1/2 cup dairy sour cream
1/2 cup cottage cheese
1 (3-oz.) pkg. cream cheese
1 (5-1/2-oz.) pkg. Noodles Romanoff,
    prepared according to package directions

In 2-quart casserole cook beef on High for 4 minutes, stirring once to break up chunks of beef. Drain excess fat. Add tomato sauce, salt and pepper. Cook on High for 5 minutes. Combine onions, green pepper, sour cream and cheeses. In 7-1/2" x 12" utility dish, layer half the noodles, all the cheese mixture and the remaining noodles. Top with meat-sauce mixture. Cover with wax paper. Cook on High for 10 minutes. Makes 6 servings.

Beef-Noodle Casserole

Meat and cheese combine for protein richness.

2 cups cooked green noodles
1/4 cup butter or margarine
1/4 cup Parmesan cheese
2 tablespoons salad oil
3/4 cup chopped onion
2 garlic cloves, crushed
1-1/2 lbs. lean ground beef
1/2 cup water

2 tablespoons sherry wine
1 tablespoon Worcestershire sauce
2 beef-bouillon cubes
1 teaspoon salt
1/4 teaspoon pepper
2 cups grated Gouda or Cheddar cheese
1/4 cup grated Parmesan cheese

Place noodles in 7-1/2" x 12" utility dish. Warm on High for 1-1/2 minutes. Add butter or margarine and 1/4 cup Parmesan cheese. Toss well. Combine oil with onion and garlic in 4-quart casserole. Cook on High for 3 minutes. Stir in beef. Cook on High for 4 minutes. Add water, sherry, Worcestershire sauce, bouillon cubes, salt and pepper. Cook on High for 3 minutes. Stir 1-1/2 cups Gouda or Cheddar cheese into meat mixture. Pour into noodle-lined casserole. Cover with wax paper. Cook on High for 8 minutes. Sprinkle with remaining Gouda or Cheddar cheese and 1/4 cup Parmesan cheese. Heat until bubbly hot. Makes 6 servings.

 *Tip* — *Warm lemons, limes, oranges or grapefruit on High for 15 seconds to release more juice and flavor. Let stand 3 minutes before squeezing.*

Italian Macaroni and Cheese

Prepare this superb supper ahead of time and reheat.

2 cups (8-oz.) mostaccioli,
  cooked and drained
3 tablespoons butter
3/4 cup chopped onion
1/3 cup chopped celery
1 or 2 garlic cloves, minced
2 (6-oz.) cans tomato paste
2 cups water

1 teaspoon basil, crushed
1 teaspoon oregano, crushed
2 teaspoons salt
1/2 teaspoon sugar
1/2 teaspoon pepper
2/3 cup grated Parmesan cheese
2 cups ricotta cheese (1-lb.)

Cook mostaccioli on cooktop according to package directions. Combine butter, onion, celery and garlic in 1-1/2-quart casserole. Cook on High for 3 to 4 minutes, stirring occasionally. Add tomato paste, water and seasonings. Cover and bring to a boil on High for about 10 minutes. Uncover. Cook on High for an additional 5 minutes. In 2-quart oblong utility dish, spread a thin layer of sauce over the bottom. Sprinkle with 1/3 of Parmesan cheese. Soften ricotta cheese on Low for 1 to 2 minutes. Layer with half each of mostaccioli, ricotta cheese, sauce and half of remaining Parmesan cheese. Repeat layers. Bake on Medium for 20 to 25 minutes or until hot and bubbly, rotating 1/2 turn after 10 minutes. Raise shelf. Brown 3 to 5 minutes until golden brown. Makes 6 servings.

Combine butter, onion, celery and garlic; sauté with Microwave on High until transparent. Add remaining sauce ingredients and simmer to blend flavors.

Confetti Meatball Supper

An easy-to-make ring mold gives eye appeal.

1 (10-oz.) pkg. frozen mixed vegetables
3 cups cooked rice
2 tablespoons melted butter or margarine
24 Basic Meatballs, page 47
1/2 cup finely chopped onion

1 (10-3/4-oz.) can condensed cream-
    of-mushroom soup
1 (11-oz.) can condensed Cheddar-cheese soup
1/2 cup catsup
2 tablespoons Worcestershire sauce

Pierce mixed-vegetable package and cook on High for 4 minutes. Drain. Mix with cooked rice and butter or margarine. Press into 5-1/2-inch ceramic ring mold. In 7-1/2" x 12" utility dish, cook meatballs and onion on High for 5 minutes. Drain excess fat. Mix soups, catsup and Worcestershire sauce. Pour over meatballs. Cover with wax paper. Cook on High for 10 minutes. Unmold rice ring on ceramic serving platter. Cover with wax paper. Heat on High 4 minutes. Arrange meatballs a-round rice mold. Pour some of sauce over meatballs and rice. Pass remaining sauce. Makes 6 servings.

New England Meat Pie

A complete meal from your cupboard and freezer.

1 lb. lean ground beef
1 egg, slightly beaten
1/4 cup fine, dry bread crumbs
2 tablespoons milk
1 teaspoon salt
1 (10-oz.) pkg. frozen mixed vegetables,
    partially thawed

1/4 teaspoon thyme
1/4 teaspoon pepper
1 (8-oz.) can tomato sauce
1 (12-oz.) pkg. frozen hash-brown
    potatoes, thawed
2 tablespoons salad oil
1/4 cup grated cheese

Combine beef with egg, bread crumbs, milk and salt. Shape into 1-inch balls. Place on metal rack in 7-1/2" x 12" utility dish. Cover. Cook on High for 5 minutes. Drain. Combine with vegetables, thyme, pepper and tomato sauce. Press potatoes on bottom and sides of regular 10-inch pie plate or deep 9-inch pie dish. Drizzle with oil. Heat on High for 3 minutes. Brown 5 minutes. Spoon meatball mixture over potatoes. Cook on High for 5 minutes. Sprinkle with cheese. Heat for 30 seconds. Makes 5 servings.

Tip

Prepare meat for dinner first. Let it stand to continue cooking while the vegetables cook.

Ruth's Shell Casserole

A dish fit for a party!

1 lb. lean ground beef
1 small onion, chopped
1/4 cup flour
1 teaspoon salt
1 teaspoon Worcestershire sauce
1/4 teaspoon garlic powder

1 (10-1/2-oz.) can beef-bouillon soup
1 (2-oz.) can sliced mushrooms, drained
2 cups cooked large shell-shaped macaroni
1 cup dairy sour cream
2 tablespoons red wine
Finely chopped parsley

In 4-quart casserole, break up beef with fork. Add onion. Cook on High for 4 minutes. Stir in flour, salt, Worcestershire sauce and garlic powder. Mix well. Add soup, mushrooms and cooked macaroni. Cover. Cook on High for 5 minutes, stirring once. Add sour cream and wine. Heat on High for 1 to 1-1/2 minutes. Sprinkle with parsley. Makes 4 to 5 servings.

Swedish Cabbage Rolls

This tasty, economical meal uses leftover rice.

12 large cabbage leaves
2 tablespoons water
1 egg
2/3 cup milk
1/4 cup finely chopped onion
1 teaspoon Worcestershire sauce

1 lb. lean ground beef
3/4 cup cooked rice
1 (10-1/2-oz.) can condensed tomato soup
1/4 cup catsup
1 tablespoon brown sugar
1 tablespoon lemon juice

Place cabbage leaves in 4-quart casserole with 2 tablespoons water. Cover. Cook on High for 6 minutes. Set aside. In bowl, combine egg, milk, onion and Worcestershire sauce. Mix well. Add beef and rice to egg mixture and beat together with fork. Trim thick parts of cabbage leaves so you can roll them without tearing. Spoon 1/4 cup of meat mixture on each leaf. Fold in sides and roll leaf ends over meat. Secure with toothpicks. Place rolls in 7-1/2" x 12" utility dish. Combine soup, catsup, brown sugar and lemon juice. Pour over cabbage rolls. Cover with plastic wrap. Cook on High for 12 minutes. Let stand 5 minutes before serving. Makes 4 servings.

Knockwurst and Hot German-Potato Salad

A winner with or without the meat.

3 medium potatoes
4 slices bacon, diced
1 small onion, diced
1 tablespoon flour
1 tablespoon sugar
1 teaspoon dry mustard
1 teaspoon salt

1/4 teaspoon pepper
1/2 cup water
1/4 cup vinegar
1/2 teaspoon celery seeds
4 knockwurst
1 tablespoon finely chopped parsley

Wash potatoes; dry and cut in half. Place in plastic bag, cut side down. Leave end of bag open. Cook on High for 10 minutes or until tender. Remove skins and slice. Cook bacon and onion in 4-cup measure on High for 4 to 5 minutes. Stir in flour, sugar, mustard, salt and pepper. Mix well. Add water, vinegar and celery seeds. Cook on High another 4 minutes, stirring once. Set aside. Make several cuts in plastic bag containing knockwurst and place bag on paper plate. Cook on High for 1-1/2 minutes. Cut each knockwurst into 6 pieces. Arrange knockwurst pieces and cooked potatoes in shallow bowl. Add hot sauce. Toss to coat evenly. Sprinkle with chopped parsley. Serve immediately. Makes 4 servings.

Beef Stroganoff

An elegant freezer-to-table dinner. Add sour cream before serving.

1/4 cup butter or margarine
1-1/2 lbs. beef sirloin, cut in 1/2" x 2" strips
1/4 cup flour
1 beef-bouillon cube
3/4 cup boiling water
1 small onion, chopped

1/4 lb. fresh mushrooms, sliced
2 tablespoons tomato paste
1 teaspoon Worcestershire sauce
3/4 teaspoon salt
1 cup dairy sour cream, room temperature

In 4-quart casserole, melt butter or margarine on High for 40 seconds. Coat beef with flour, then with melted butter or margarine. Cook, uncovered, on High for 3 minutes. Stir. Cook another 2 minutes. Dissolve bouillon cube in boiling water. Add bouillon, onion, mushrooms, tomato paste, Worcestershire sauce and salt to meat. Stir. Cover. Cook on High for 5 minutes. Let stand 4 minutes. Uncover. Stir in sour cream. Heat on High for 1 to 1-1/2 minutes. Makes 4 servings.

Knockwurst and Hot German-Potato Salad

Tip — To peel fresh peaches or tomatoes easily, heat on High for 10 to 20 seconds, according to size and quantity. Then let stand for 10 minutes before peeling.

Chili

...hat's tasty enough for company.

1 lb. ground beef
1/2 cup chopped green pepper
1 tablespoon instant onion
2 (16-oz.) cans dark-red kidney
   beans, drained

1 (16-oz.) can tomatoes, cut up
1 (8-oz.) can tomato sauce
1 teaspoon seasoned salt
1 pkg. chili seasoning

In 4-quart casserole, cook meat, green pepper and onion on High for 5 minutes or until vegetables are tender, stirring once. Stir in remaining ingredients. Cover. Cook on High for 15 minutes, stirring once. Makes 6 servings.

Variation:
To make chili more spicy, substitute 2 (16-ounce) cans of chili beans with sauce for dark-red kidney beans.

Chili Steaks

A sophisticated version of chili and beans.

2 tablespoons flour
1 teaspoon chili powder
1-1/2 lbs. round steak, cut into 4 or 5 pieces
2 tablespoons salad oil
1 onion, sliced

1 (8-oz.) can tomatoes
1 (15-oz.) can chili with beans
1 teaspoon salt
1/2 cup grated Cheddar cheese

Combine flour and chili powder in plastic or paper bag. Pound meat and add to bag. Shake until coated. Pour oil in a 7-1/2" x 12" utility dish. Heat on High for 1-1/2 minutes. Add meat; turn to coat both sides with hot oil. Cook on High 4 minutes. Stir. Add onion, tomatoes, chili with beans and salt. Cover with wax paper. Cook on Low for 25 minutes, stirring once. Uncover; sprinkle with cheese. Cook on High for another 30 seconds. Makes 4 servings.

Spoonburgers

Keep buns and sauce in the freezer for unexpected company.

1-1/2 lbs. lean ground beef
1 medium onion, chopped
1 (10-1/2-oz.) can condensed tomato soup
2 tablespoons water
1 tablespoon vinegar
1 tablespoon brown sugar

1 teaspoon chili powder
1 teaspoon Worcestershire sauce
1/2 teaspoon salt
1/4 teaspoon celery salt
5 or 6 hamburger buns

In 4-quart casserole, cook beef and onion on High for 6 minutes, stirring twice. Combine remaining ingredients except buns and pour over meat. Cover. Cook on High for 4 minutes. Warm all hamburger buns on Low for 1-1/2 minutes. Spoon sauce over buns and serve. Makes 4 to 5 servings.

Tacos

A treat for the young and young-at-heart.

1 lb. lean ground beef
1 (1-1/4-oz.) pkg. taco-seasoning mix
1/2 cup hot water
6 or 7 cooked taco shells

2 cups shredded lettuce
2 medium tomatoes, chopped
Grated cheese

In 2-quart casserole, crumble beef. Cook on High for 4 minutes, stirring once. Drain fat; stir in dry taco-seasoning mix and water. Cover lightly with paper towel. Cook on High for 5 minutes, stirring once. Heat cooked taco shells on paper towel or paper plate on High for 30 seconds. Fill shells with ground-beef mixture, lettuce, tomatoes and cheese. Makes 6 or 7 tacos.

Oriental Supper

Oriental vegetables dress up meatballs and gravy.

24 Basic Meatballs, page 47
1 (10-1/2-oz.) can condensed beef broth
1 soup-can hot water
1 medium onion, sliced
1-1/2 cups bias-sliced celery (1/2-inch pieces)
1 (16-oz.) can chop-suey vegetables, drained

1 (6-oz.) can mushrooms
3 tablespoons cornstarch
1/2 cup cold water
3 tablespoons soy sauce
1 (3-oz.) can chow-mein noodles

In 7-1/2" x 12" utility dish, cook meatballs on High for 5 minutes. Add beef broth and soup-can of hot water. Stir in onion and celery. Cover with wax paper. Cook on High for 8 minutes. Add chop-suey vegetables and mushrooms. Blend cornstarch with 1/2 cup cold water and soy sauce. Stir into casserole. Cover. Cook on High for 5 minutes or until mixture thickens, stirring several times. Serve over chow-mein noodles. Makes 4 to 5 servings.

Fiesta Bake

A taste adventure with traditional tamale pie.

1 qt. Basic Meat Sauce, page 50
1 teaspoon chili powder
1 (12-oz.) can whole-kernel corn, not drained
1 (8-1/2-oz.) pkg. corn-muffin mix

1 egg
1/3 cup milk
1 teaspoon sugar
Chopped chives

Mix Basic Meat Sauce with chili powder and corn. Stir into 7-1/2" x 12" utility dish. Cover with wax paper. Cook on High for 3 minutes. Uncover. In the meantime, combine muffin mix with egg, milk and sugar. Drop by tablespoon on top of hot meat-sauce mixture. Sprinkle with chives. Raise shelf. Cook on High for 5 minutes, turning dish once. Brown 3 to 5 minutes. Makes 6 servings.

Hacienda Holiday Casserole

Use the sauce from your freezer for a meal in a jiffy.

1 qt. Basic Meat Sauce, page 50
1 cup refried beans
2 tablespoons chopped green chiles

6 tortillas
1 (2-1/4-oz.) can sliced ripe olives, drained
2 cups grated Cheddar cheese

In 2-quart casserole, combine Basic Meat Sauce with refried beans and chiles. Arrange alternate layers of sauce with tortillas, olives and cheese. Cook on High for 7 minutes, turning casserole once. Makes 4 servings.

Corned Beef and Cabbage

The convenience of fast cooking with slow-cooked flavor.

3-lb.-round of corned beef in package
  with seasonings
3 medium potatoes, peeled and quartered

3 carrots, quartered
1 small head cabbage, cut into wedges

Place the corned beef and seasonings in large roasting bag tied with a string or rubber band. Set roasting bag inside 4-quart casserole. Cook on Low for 20 minutes. Turn dish. Cook a second 20 minutes. Open bag, add potatoes and carrots, close bag. Cook on Low for a third 20 minutes. Add cabbage to bag. Cook on Low for 15 minutes or until vegetables are tender. Let stand covered for 10 minutes. Makes 6 servings.

Mandarin-Style Steak

Exotic sauce and textures for a festive occasion.

1-1/2 lbs. round steak, about 1/2-inch thick
2 tablespoons salad oil
1 (1-3/8-oz.) envelope onion-soup mix
2 tablespoons soy sauce
1/4 teaspoon ground ginger
1 cup water

1 (8-1/2-oz.) can water chestnuts,
  drained and sliced
1/2 green pepper, sliced
1 tomato, cut into wedges
2 tablespoons toasted sesame seeds

Cut steak into 1/4-inch-wide strips. In 4-quart casserole, heat oil on High for 1-1/2 minutes. Add meat. Cook on High for 3 minutes. Stir. Cook 1-1/2 minutes. Stir in soup mix, soy sauce, ginger and water. Cover. Cook on Low for 25 minutes or until tender. Stir in water chestnuts, green pepper and tomato. Cook on High for 1 minute. Let stand 10 minutes before serving. Garnish with sesame seeds. Serve with crisp Chinese noodles. Makes 4 to 5 servings.

Clockwise from top right: Hacienda Holiday Casserole, Corned Beef and Cabbage, Fiesta Bake, Oriental Supper, Tacos.

Country Garden Bake

A tasty meal from your pantry and freezer.

2 lbs. lean ground beef
1 garlic clove, crushed
1 cup chopped onion
Salt and pepper
1 (10-oz.) pkg. frozen Mexican corn
   with butter sauce

1 (10-oz.) pkg. frozen peas in butter sauce
1 (3-oz.) can sliced mushrooms, drained
2 tablespoons butter or margarine
Instant mashed potatoes, servings for 4
4 tablespoons grated Romano cheese
1/4 cup grated Cheddar cheese

In 2-quart casserole, break up meat with fork. Add garlic and onion. Cook on High for 7 to 8 minutes. Sprinkle with salt and pepper. Pierce packages and thaw corn and peas in packages on High for 4 to 7 minutes. Add the corn, peas, mushrooms and butter or margarine to meat mixture. Stir until butter is melted. Cover. Cook on High for 6 minutes. While meat mixture is cooking, prepare instant potatoes according to package directions for 4 servings. Spoon potatoes over casserole. Raise shelf. Heat on High for 2 minutes. Sprinkle with cheeses. Brown 4 to 6 minutes. Makes 6 servings.

Meatball Garden Dish

A hearty variation of meatball stew.

24 Basic Meatballs, page 47
1 (10-1/2-oz.) can condensed beef broth
1 soup-can hot water
3 medium potatoes, peeled and quartered
6 medium carrots, peeled, quartered
   and halved

1 medium onion, sliced
1 (10-oz.) pkg. frozen peas
1/3 cup flour
2/3 cup cold water
Salt and pepper to taste

In 4-quart casserole, cook Basic Meatballs on High for 5 minutes, stirring once. Pour in broth and soup-can of hot water. Add potatoes, carrots and onion. Cover. Cook on High for 15 to 20 minutes or until vegetables are tender. With slotted spoon remove meat and vegetables and place in serving dish. Thaw peas in pierced package on High for 4 minutes. Add to meat and vegetable mixture. Stir flour into drippings left in 4-quart casserole. Add cold water and salt and pepper to taste. Cook on High for 5 minutes or until gravy thickens, stirring often. Pour part of gravy over vegetables and meat. Pass remaining gravy. Makes 6 servings.

Pizza Burgers

Flavorful pizza sauce over stuffed hamburgers.

2 lbs. lean ground beef
1/2 cup grated mozzarella cheese
1/4 cup chopped ripe olives
2 tablespoons grated Parmesan cheese
1 teaspoon instant minced onion

1/2 teaspoon salt
1 (8-oz.) can pizza sauce
1/2 teaspoon oregano
1/2 teaspoon garlic salt

Divide meat into 4 large patties about 6-inches in diameter. Combine mozzarella, olives, Parmesan cheese, onion and salt. Place 1/4 of cheese mixture in center of each burger. Fold burgers over; press edges together. Place on metal rack in 7-1/2" x 12" utility dish. Cook on High for 4 minutes. Turn dish. Cook for 2 minutes. Rearrange meat on rack. Cook 2 to 4 minutes, depending on desired doneness. In 2-cup measure, combine pizza sauce with oregano and garlic salt. Heat on High for 3 minutes. Serve with burgers. Makes 4 generous servings.

Beef Enchiladas with Cheese

Assembling enchiladas can be a family affair.

1 lb. lean ground beef
1 cup grated Monterey Jack or
   Cheddar cheese
1 (2-1/2-oz.) can sliced ripe olives, drained
1 (6-oz.) can tomato paste

1 (1-5/8-oz.) pkg. enchilada-sauce mix
3 cups warm water
8 corn tortillas
1-1/2 cups grated Monterey Jack or
   Cheddar cheese

In 2-quart casserole, crumble beef. Cook on High for 4 minutes, stirring twice. Drain fat. Add 1 cup cheese and olives to meat. In 2-1/2-quart casserole, blend tomato paste with enchilada-sauce mix. Stir in water. Cover. Cook on High for 8 minutes. Pour 1 cup prepared enchilada sauce in 7-1/2" x 12" utility dish. Dip each tortilla into remaining heated sauce. Spoon meat mixture in center of each tortilla. Fold sides of tortilla over filling and place in baking dish, seam side down. Pour remaining sauce over filled tortillas. Top with 1-1/2 cups cheese. Cover with plastic wrap. Heat on High for 3 minutes. Turn dish. Cook another 3 minutes. Makes 8 enchiladas.

Spanish Stuffed Onions

The beef-and-onion combination is always a winner.

4 large onions, peeled
   (about 1-1/2 lbs.)
1/4 cup water
1/2 lb. lean ground beef
1 (8-oz.) can tomato sauce

1 cup cooked rice
1 teaspoon chili powder
1/2 teaspoon salt
Dash pepper
1/2 cup shredded Cheddar cheese

Place onions and water in 2-quart casserole. Cover. Cook on High for 8 to 9 minutes or until onions are just about tender. Drain. Scoop out centers of onions, leaving walls about 1/3-inch thick. Chop enough onion pulp to make 1/2 cup. Combine with ground beef in 1-quart casserole. Cook, covered, on High for 3 to 4 minutes. Drain off fat. Stir in half tomato sauce and all remaining ingredients except cheese. Stuff onions with beef-rice mixture, mounding high on top. Spoon any remaining mixture in dish around onions. Pour remaining tomato sauce over all. Cook on High for 6 minutes. Sprinkle cheese on top. Continue to cook on High for 1 to 2 minutes or until cheese melts. Makes 4 servings.

Cook onions in covered dish until just tender. Scoop out centers. Mound meat and rice mixture high in onion shells, top with tomato sauce and cheese.

Vegetables

You'll soon prefer to cook fresh vegetables in your microwave oven—not only because it's faster, but also because vegetables look more appealing, taste better and have higher nutritive value. You'll also appreciate the convenience of cooking vegetables in their own skins or in serving dishes or containers.

Wash, trim and then cook vegetables in a very small amount of water, as indicated on the Vegetable Cooking Table, page 119, or with only the moisture that clings from washing. When cooking in water, always use a lid, or cover with plastic wrap or wax paper. Exceptions are potatoes and squash; they are cooked in their skins. Simply pierce the skin, place the vegetables on a paper towel, allow a 1-inch space around each one and cook.

Choose a dish with a size and shape similar to the size and shape of the vegetable. For example, cook a whole head of cauliflower in a pie plate covered with plastic wrap. Cook broccoli spears on a heat-tempered glass pizza platter with the stems toward the edge and the flowerettes towards the center, covered with plastic.

The cooking times on the Vegetable Cooking Table, page 119, are for crisp-tender or slightly-firm vegetables. Vegetables continue to cook during the standing time and become tender and succulent. Quick-cooking in a small amount of water retains more of the flower and water-soluable vitamins. Add salt after cooking or to the cooking water to avoid drying the vegetable. Add herbs to the cooking water, if desired.

Fresh vegetables cook at different speeds depending on density as shown on the Vegetable Cooking Table, page 119. If you combine two or more vegetables for cooking, you have to compensate for the cooking-time difference. One way is to cut the longer-cooking vegetable into smaller pieces. Or you can vary cooking times. For example, a stew calls for potatoes, carrots, onions and mushrooms during the last five minutes of cooking.

Canned vegetables are partially cooked so they heat quickly and easily. Drain off most of the liquid, remove from the can, put in a cooking dish, cover and heat on High for about 1-1/2 to 2 minutes per cupful. Stir once to move vegetables from the edge to the center.

Cook frozen vegetables in the package, but always pierce the package to let steam escape.

See Vegetable Cooking Table, page 119.

Corn Bake

A zesty vegetable dish with protein, too.

2 (12-oz.) cans whole-kernel corn, drained
1 (6-oz.) can evaporated milk
1 egg, beaten
1 tablespoon minced onion
1 tablespoon diced pimiento
1/2 cup shredded Monterey Jack or
    Cheddar cheese

1/2 teaspoon salt
1 tablespoon butter
1/2 cup soft bread crumbs
1/4 cup shredded Monterey Jack or
    Cheddar cheese

In 7-1/2" x 12" utility dish, combine corn and milk with egg, onion, pimiento, 1/2 cup cheese and salt. In 1-cup measure, melt butter on High for 35 seconds. Stir in bread crumbs and 1/4 cup cheese. Set aside. Cover casserole with wax paper. Raise shelf. Cook on High for 3 minutes. Turn dish. Cook another 2 minutes. Sprinkle with crumb topping. Heat 1 minute. Remove paper. Brown 5 minutes. Makes 6 servings.

Harvard Beets

Add zip to a buffet or dinner.

2 tablespoons butter or margarine
1/4 cup sugar
1 tablespoon cornstarch
1/4 teaspoon salt

1/4 cup vinegar
1/4 cup beet juice, drained from canned beets
2 cups canned shoestring, cubed or
    sliced beets, drained

In 2-quart casserole, melt butter or margarine on High for 1 minute. Mix sugar and cornstarch together. Add salt. Stir into melted butter until smooth. Add vinegar and beet juice. Cook on High for 2 to 3 minutes, or until clear. Add drained beets. Cover. Heat on High for 4 minutes. Makes 4 servings.

Pickled Beets and Eggs, Cracker-Barrel Style

Take them along on your next picnic.

5 fresh beets
1/2 cup water
1/2 cup vinegar
1/2 cup cold water
1/4 cup brown sugar, firmly packed

1/2 teaspoon salt
1 small stick cinnamon
3 whole cloves
6 hard-cooked eggs, peeled

Wash beets and trim stocks. Place beets in 2-quart casserole and add water. Cover. Cook on High for 12 minutes. Let stand, covered, while making sauce. Measure vinegar and cold water into 2-cup measure. Add brown sugar, salt, cinnamon and cloves. Drain beets. Slip off skins. Pour sauce over beets. Cover. Cook on High for 8 minutes. Let stand several days. Remove beets from sauce. Add eggs to sauce. Cover. Let pickle in refrigerator for 2 days before using. Makes 5 pickled beets and 6 pickled eggs.

Chilled Asparagus Vinaigrette

Chilled vegetables add sophistication to a dinner.

1 lb. fresh asparagus spears
1/4 cup water

Sauce:

Cooking liquid from asparagus spears
   with water to make 1/2 cup liquid
1/4 cup cider vinegar
2 teaspoons parsley
2 teaspoons chives

2 teaspoons pimiento
2 teaspoons capers
1 teaspoon salt
1/2 teaspoon dry mustard
1/8 teaspoon pepper

Cut off or snap off the lower part of spears. If desired, peel spears with vegetable peeler. Place in rectangular baking dish, alternating the direction of half the spears. Add 1/4 cup water. Cover with plastic wrap. Cook on High for 4 minutes. Rearrange spears, moving the inside ones to the outside of dish. Cook on High for 3 minutes. Drain. Reserve liquid for sauce. Prepare sauce and pour over asparagus spears. Place in refrigerator to marinate 12 hours or overnight. To serve, drain off liquid, reserving the parsley, chives, capers and pimientos as garnish. Makes 4 servings.

Sauce:
Put all the ingredients in a screw-top jar. Cover jar tightly. Shake to blend well. Makes about 3/4 cup.

Variation:
Use 1 (10-oz.) package of frozen asparagus instead of fresh, if desired. See Vegetable Cooking Table, page 119, for cooking instructions.

Green Beans Supreme

Prepare these during the roast's standing time.

2 tablespoons butter or margarine
2 tablespoons flour
1 tablespoon instant minced onion
1/4 teaspoon salt
1/2 teaspoon grated lemon peel
1/4 teaspoon pepper

1/4 cup water
1 cup dairy sour cream, room temperature
2 (16-oz.) cans green beans, drained
2 tablespoons butter or margarine
1/2 cup dry bread crumbs
1/4 cup grated Cheddar cheese

In 4-cup measure, melt 2 tablespoons butter or margarine on High for 30 seconds. Stir in flour, onion, salt, lemon peel and pepper. Cook on High for 1 minute. Stir in water, then sour cream. Mix with green beans. Spoon into 2-quart casserole. In 2-cup measure, melt 2 tablespoons butter or margarine on High for 30 seconds. Stir in bread crumbs and cheese. Set aside. Raise shelf. Cook casserole on High for 5 minutes. Sprinkle bread-crumb topping over casserole. Heat on High for 1 minute. Brown 4 minutes. Makes 6 to 7 servings.

Marie's Tomato Stack-ups

A colorful combination.

1 (10-oz.) pkg. frozen spinach or broccoli,
   drained and chopped
3 large tomatoes

1/4 teaspoon salt
1/2 cup grated Swiss cheese
1/4 cup minced onion

Make 2 knife slits on top of spinach or broccoli package. Cook in package on High for 6 minutes. Set aside. Cut the tomatoes in half. Sprinkle lightly with salt. Set aside 1/4 cup of the grated cheese. Combine remaining cheese, spinach and onion. Place tomato halves in 7-1/2" x 12" utility dish. Mound vegetable mixture onto the tomatoes. Raise shelf. Cook on High for 4 minutes. Sprinkle with cheese. Brown 5 minutes. Makes 6 servings.

Broccoli-Onion Bouquets

A gentle blend of vegetable flavors.

4 medium white onions
1 lb. broccoli

1/2 cup chicken stock
Salt and pepper

Peel onions and cut 1-inch core from center. Wash and trim broccoli. Use flowerettes. Place broccoli and cored onions separately in the same casserole. Add chicken stock. Cover. Cook on High for 6 minutes. Place broccoli flowerettes in cored onions. After cooking, broccoli should fit snugly in cored onions. Cover. Cook on High for 3 minutes. Sprinkle with salt and pepper. Makes 4 servings.

Spinach-Cheese Bake

Serve this for compliments galore.

1 (10-oz.) pkg. frozen chopped spinach
2 tablespoons flour
2 eggs, beaten
1 (3-oz.) pkg. cream cheese, cubed
3/4 cup cubed American cheese
1/4 cup butter, cubed

1-1/2 teaspoons instant minced onion
1/2 teaspoon salt
1/2 cup fine bread crumbs
1/4 cup butter
1/3 cup Parmesan cheese

In 1-1/2-quart covered dish, cook spinach on High for 6 minutes, stirring once half-way through. Drain. Stir in flour, then eggs, cheeses, cubed butter, onion and salt. Mix well. Cook on High for 9 to 11 minutes, stirring twice. Remove from oven. Measure bread crumbs into a 1-cup measure. Add 1/4 cup butter. Heat on High until butter is melted, about 1 minute. Stir until crumbs are well coated with butter. Sprinkle over the spinach mixture. Top with Parmesan cheese. Raise shelf. Brown as desired. Makes 4 servings.

Creamy Cabbage

Rich butter sauce enhances the cabbage flavor.

1/4 cup butter
1/2 small head cabbage, shredded,
   about 1 quart
1/4 cup light cream

1/4 teaspoon salt
1/4 teaspoon seasoned salt
1/8 teaspoon pepper

In 2-quart casserole, melt butter on High for 40 seconds. Add cabbage, stirring to coat with butter. Cover. Cook on High for 2 minutes. Stir in cream. Cover. Cook on High for 3 minutes, stirring once. Sprinkle with salt, seasoned salt and pepper. Let stand several minutes before serving. Makes 4 servings.

Scalloped Potatoes

All the more interesting with the subtle flavor of Swiss cheese.

3 to 3-1/2 cups raw boiling potatoes,
   peeled and thinly sliced
3/4 cup grated Swiss cheese
1/2 cup milk

2 tablespoons butter or margarine
1/2 teaspoon onion salt
1/4 teaspoon pepper

Butter 2-quart casserole. Place half of the potatoes in the casserole, top with half of the cheese, then the rest of the potatoes. In 2-cup measure, heat milk, butter or margarine and seasonings on High for 2 minutes. Pour over casserole. Raise shelf. Cover. Cook on High for 10 to 12 minutes or until crisp and tender. Top with remaining cheese. Remove cover. Brown 5 to 6 minutes. Makes 4 servings.

Sunshine Potatoes

An old standard takes on a new glow.

1/4 cup butter or margarine, melted
1 tablespoon fresh-squeezed lemon juice
3 large potatoes, thinly sliced
2 teaspoons fresh-grated lemon peel

3 tablespoons grated Parmesan cheese
1/2 teaspoon paprika
Lemon wedges

Combine melted butter or margarine and lemon juice. Arrange potato slices in 7-1/2" x 12" utility dish. Brush cut surfaces of potatoes with lemon-butter mixture. Combine lemon peel, cheese and paprika. Sprinkle over potatoes. Raise shelf. Cover dish with plastic wrap. Cook on High for 10 to 12 minutes. Remove cover. Brown 5 to 6 minutes. Serve with lemon wedges. Makes 4 servings.

Orange-Glazed Sweet Potatoes

Sweet-potato goodness in thick, golden sauce.

3 large, cooked sweet potatoes or
   1 (29-oz.) can, drained
1/3 cup brown sugar, firmly packed
1 tablespoon cornstarch

1/3 cup orange juice
1/2 teaspoon grated orange peel
1/4 teaspoon salt
2 tablespoons butter or margarine

Peel potatoes and cut into halves. If potatoes are large, cut into quarters. In 4-cup measure, combine sugar with cornstarch. Stir in orange juice, orange peel and salt. Cook on High for 2-1/2 to 3 minutes, stirring twice. Add butter or margarine to glaze. If thinner glaze is desired, add more orange juice. Arrange potatoes in 2-quart casserole. Pour sauce over potatoes. Cook on High 5 to 6 minutes. Makes 4 to 5 servings.

Variations:

Yams may be substituted for sweet potatoes. For marshmallow topping, sprinkle top of casserole with marshmallows after cooking. Raise shelf. Heat on High for 1 minute. Brown 3 to 5 minutes, turning dish once.

Potatoes Au Gratin

Remember, potatoes cook fast in a microwave oven.

4 medium potatoes
1/4 cup butter or margarine
1/4 cup flour
2 cups milk
1/2 teaspoon seasoned salt

1/8 teaspoon pepper
1 cup grated Cheddar cheese
1 onion, thinly sliced
1/2 cup grated Parmesan cheese
Paprika

Wash potatoes. Dry and cut in half crosswise. Place in plastic bag, cut side down. Leave end of bag open. Cook on High for 10 minutes. Remove skins and slice. In 4-cup glass measure, melt butter or margarine on High for 40 seconds. Stir in flour, then milk, seasoned salt and pepper. Cook on High for 3-1/2 minutes, or until mixture thickens, stirring twice. Blend in Cheddar cheese. Place cooked potatoes and onion in 7-1/2" x 12" utility dish. Add sauce. Stir. Cover with wax paper. Raise shelf. Cook on High for 6 minutes. Exact cooking time depends on thickness of potatoes. Top with Parmesan cheese and paprika. Brown 5 minutes. Makes 4 servings.

Tomatoes Parmesan

Cook them right on the serving platter.

2 medium tomatoes
2 tablespoons grated Parmesan cheese
2 tablespoons fine, dry bread crumbs
1 tablespoon melted butter or margarine

1 teaspoon chopped chives
1/8 teaspoon paprika
Dash of cayenne pepper
Dash of MSG

Cut tomatoes in half and place in 2-quart casserole. Combine the remaining ingredients and spoon over tomatoes. Raise shelf. Cook on High for 1-1/2 to 2 minutes. Brown 4 to 5 minutes. Makes 4 servings.

Glazed Carrots

Crisp and tender carrots in a tangy sauce.

6 carrots, peeled and sliced crosswise
2 tablespoons water
2 tablespoons butter or margarine

1/4 cup brown sugar, firmly packed
1/4 teaspoon salt
1 teaspoon prepared mustard

In 2-quart casserole, cook carrots in water on High for 9 to 10 minutes, stirring twice. Drain, cover and set aside. In a 1-cup measure, melt butter or margarine on High for 30 seconds. Stir in brown sugar, salt and mustard. Pour over drained carrots. Cover. Heat on High for 2 minutes. Makes 4 servings.

Stuffed Zucchini

A new look for a traditional vegetable.

4 medium zucchini
2 tablespoons water
1 (6-oz.) pkg. chicken-flavored stuffing mix

1-3/4 cups water
1/4 cup butter or margarine

In 7-1/2" x 12" utility dish, place whole zucchini with 2 tablespoons water. Cover with wax paper. Cook on High for 10 to 12 minutes, turning dish once. Cool slightly. Cut in half, lengthwise. Scoop out centers and save. In 4-cup measure, combine seasoning packet from package of stuffing mix with 1-3/4 cup water and butter or margarine. Cook on High for 3 to 4 minutes. Cover and let stand 5 minutes. Stir in bread crumbs from mix to moisten. Add scooped-out zucchini centers. Spoon into cooked zucchini shells. Heat in 7-1/2" x 12" utility dish on High for 4 to 6 minutes. Makes 8 servings.

Top to bottom: Tomatoes Parmesan, Stuffed Zucchini, Glazed Carrots.

Mixed Vegetable Medley

The sauce is a serving-stretcher.

2 (10-oz.) pkgs. frozen, mixed vegetables
3 tablespoons butter
2 tablespoons flour

1 cup light cream or milk
1-1/2 teaspoons instant minced onion

Make two knife slits in top of vegetable package. Cook vegetables in package on High for 8 minutes. Drain and set aside. In 2-quart casserole, melt butter on High for 35 seconds. Blend in flour, then gradually stir in cream or milk. Cook on High for 1 minute. Stir. Cook 2 minutes. Add onion and drained vegetables. Makes 6 servings.

Hot Bean Trio

Serve this terrific combination hot or cold.

4 slices bacon
1/3 cup sugar
1 tablespoon cornstarch
1 teaspoon salt
1/4 teaspoon pepper
1/2 cup white wine vinegar

1 onion, sliced
1 (1-lb.) can cut green beans, drained
1 (1-lb.) can cut wax beans, drained
1 (1-lb.) can kidney beans, drained
1 hard-cooked egg, sliced

Arrange bacon on metal rack in 7-1/2" x 12" utility dish. Cover with paper towel. Cook on High for 4 minutes. Set bacon aside. Bacon crisps with standing time. Remove rack. Add sugar, cornstarch, salt, pepper, vinegar and onion to bacon drippings. Cook on High for 4 to 5 minutes or until thick, stirring several times. Add beans, mixing well. Cover. Cook on High 4 to 6 minutes, stirring once. Crumble bacon and sprinkle over top. Garnish with egg. Makes 8 to 9 servings.

Quick Baked Beans

Dressed-up canned pork and beans.

4 slices bacon, diced
1/2 cup chopped onion
1 (28-oz.) can pork and beans

2 tablespoons brown sugar
1 tablespoon Worcestershire sauce
1 teaspoon prepared mustard

In 2-quart casserole, cook bacon and onion on High for 5 minutes. Drain excess fat. Add remaining ingredients. Cover. Cook on High for 8 to 10 minutes, stirring twice. Makes 5 to 6 servings.

Summer Squash Italiano

A good recipe for zucchini, too.

3 tablespoons butter or margarine
1 onion, minced
1 garlic clove, minced
1 small green pepper, chopped
Oregano to taste

1-1/2 lbs. summer squash, sliced
4 medium tomatoes, peeled and chopped
1/2 teaspoon salt
1 cup grated Parmesan cheese

In 7-1/2" x 12" utility dish, cook butter or margarine with the onion, garlic, green pepper and oregano on High for 4 minutes. Stir in squash, tomatoes and salt. Cover. Raise shelf. Cook on High for 8 minutes. Stir and check for doneness. If necessary, cook 2 more minutes. Remove cover. Top with Parmesan cheese. Brown 4 to 5 minutes. Makes 6 servings.

Fresh Vegetable Platter

Make your own vegetable combination. The variety is endless.

1 medium cauliflower, whole and cored
1 onion, quartered
3 carrots, cut in 3/4-inch slices

4 (3-inch-long) broccoli spears,
   quartered lengthwise

Wash vegetables but do not dry. Put on serving platter or in 4-quart casserole. Cover with lid or plastic wrap. Cook on High for 12 to 14 minutes, turning once. Cover and let stand for 5 minutes. Top with butter, Cheese Sauce, page 124, or Hollandaise Sauce, page 124. Makes 4 to 6 servings.

Variation:
Use any combination of fresh vegetables. For best results, select ones of equal density, or add quicker-cooking vegetables during last half of cooking time. Season to taste.

Glazed Acorn Squash

The sauce adds a gourmet touch.

2 acorn squash
1/2 cup honey
1 tablespoon lemon juice

1/4 teaspoon nutmeg
1/4 teaspoon grated lemon peel

Pierce whole squash several times and place on paper towels. Cook on High for 8 to 10 minutes or until soft. Let stand 5 minutes. Slice crosswise into 1-inch slices. Scoop out seeds. Combine remaining ingredients. Place squash in 7-1/2" x 12" utility dish. Spoon sauce over squash. Cover. Cook on High for 4 to 6 minutes or until hot. Makes 4 servings.

Variation:
Squash may be cut in half lengthwise or in half crosswise.

Zucchini and Mushrooms Gratiné

Make this ahead. Reheat the sauce later and add the sour cream.

4 medium zucchini, cut into 1-inch slices
2 tablespoons water
1/2 teaspoon dried dill
1 garlic clove
1/2 lb. fresh mushrooms, sliced

1/4 cup butter or margarine
2 tablespoons flour
1 cup dairy sour cream, room temperature
1/2 cup crumbled herb croutons
1/2 cup grated Cheddar cheese

In 4-quart casserole, combine zucchini with water, dill and garlic. Cover. Cook on High for 5 minutes. Stir in mushrooms. Cover. Cook on High for 4 minutes. Let stand, covered, while making sauce. In 7-1/2" x 12" utility dish, melt butter or margarine on High for 40 seconds. Stir in flour. Discard garlic clove from zucchini. Drain, reserving 2 tablespoons liquid. Add reserve liquid to flour and butter or margarine mixture. Stir. Cook on High for 2 minutes. Fold sour cream into sauce. Add zucchini and mushroom mixture. Cover with plastic wrap. Heat 4 minutes on High. Sprinkle with herb croutons and cheese. Remove plastic wrap. Raise shelf. Brown 4 to 5 minutes. Makes 5 to 6 servings.

Scalloped Tomatoes

Tasty vegetables in creamy sauce.

3 tablespoons butter or margarine
1/4 cup minced onion
1/4 cup minced celery
1 tablespoon sugar
1 teaspoon salt

2 tablespoons flour
1/8 teaspoon pepper
1 (28-oz.) can tomatoes, cut up
3 slices bread, toasted, buttered and
   cut into cubes

In 2-quart casserole, place butter or margarine, onion and celery. Cover. Cook on High for 3 minutes. Add sugar, salt, flour and pepper. Cook on High for 1 minute. Stir in tomatoes. Cover. Cook on High for 3 minutes. Remove cover. Top with toast cubes. Cook on High 2 minutes more. Makes 4 servings.

Variation:
Croutons may be substituted for toast cubes.

Rice with Vegetables

A gentle blend of tender rice and crunchy vegetables.

1-3/4 cups water or stock
1 cup long-grain rice
3 tablespoons butter or margarine
1/2 teaspoon salt

2 small tomatoes, chopped, discard seeds
2 green onions, chopped
2 stalks celery, chopped
6 stuffed green olives, chopped

In covered 4-quart casserole heat water to boiling on High for 4-1/2 minutes. Add rice, butter or margarine and salt. Cover. Cook on High for 10 to 11 minutes. With a fork, fold chopped vegetables into cooked rice. Let stand, covered, for 10 minutes. Makes 6 servings.

Vegetable Cooking Table

VEGETABLE	POWER SETTING AND APPROXIMATE TIMING		METHOD
	FRESH	FROZEN	
ARTICHOKES Whole, 15 oz.	High for		Wash; cut off tips of leaves. Wrap in wax paper, cooking bag, or covered dish. Let stand 5 minutes covered.
1 artichoke	5 minutes		
2 artichokes	9 minutes		
Hearts, 10-oz. pkg.		High for 4 to 5 minutes	Cook in 2 tablespoons water in covered dish. Let stand 3 minutes, covered.
ASPARAGUS Spears, 1 lb.	High for 4 to 6 minutes		Snap off lower part of spears. Peel, if desired. Alternate direction of spears in utility dish. Cover. Turn dish once. Let stand 3 to 5 minutes.
Spears, 10 oz.		High for 7 to 8 Minutes	Turn dish once. Let stand 3 to 5 minutes.
Cut, 10 oz.		High for 5 to 6 minutes	Stir once. Let stand 5 minutes, covered.
BEANS, GREEN 1 lb., Cut	High for 10 to 12 minutes with 3 tablespoons water		Add water to dish; cover. Stir twice. Let stand 5 minutes, covered.
10 oz., Cut		High for 6 to 7 minutes with 2 tablespoons water	
BEANS, LIMA 10 oz.		High for 6 to 7 minutes, ice side up	Cook in covered dish. Stir twice.
BEAN SPROUTS, 1 lb.	High for 4 to 5 minutes		Rinse; put in 4-qt. covered casserole with water that clings from rinsing. Stir halfway through cooking time. Let stand, covered, 3 minutes.
BEETS, 1 lb. Whole (about 1 bunch)	High for 11 to 13 minutes with 1/4 to 1/2 cup water		Wash; remove leaves to 1-inch from top. Cook in covered dish. Stir once. Let stand, covered, 5 minutes. Remove skin. Season.
BROCCOLI 1-1/2 lb., Spears	High for 7 to 9 minutes with 1 tablespoon water		Quarter stems. Alternate stems and flowerettes in utility dish or place stems to outside of dish. Cover. Turn once. Let stand, covered, 5 minutes.
10 oz., Spears		High for 7 to 8 minutes. ice side up	Break apart in center. Stir once. Let stand, covered, 5 minutes.
10 oz., Chopped		6 to 7 minutes, ice side up	Break apart in center. Stir once. Let stand, covered, 5 minutes.

Vegetable Cooking Table (Continued)

VEGETABLE	POWER SETTING AND APPROXIMATE TIMING		METHOD
	FRESH	FROZEN	
BRUSSEL SPROUTS 1/2 lb., Whole	High for 4 to 5 minutes with 1 tablespoon water		Wash. Cook in covered dish. Stir halfway through cooking time. Let stand, covered, 5 minutes.
10 oz.		High for 8 to 9 minutes with 2 tablespoons water	Cook, covered. Stir or break apart halfway through cooking time. Let stand, covered, 5 minutes.
CABBAGE 1-3/4 lbs. Sliced (1 small head)	High for 10 to 12 minutes with 1 tablespoon water		Rinse; slice or chop. Put in covered casserole. Stir halfway through cooking time. Let stand, covered, 5 minutes.
CARROTS, Sliced, 5 oz., (2 Medium)	High for: 4 to 5 minutes with 2 tablespoons water		
10 oz., (4 Medium)	7 to 8 minutes minutes with 2 tablespoons water		Cover. Cook. Stir halfway through cooking time. Let stand, covered, 3 minutes.
1 lb. (6 Medium)	9 to 10 minutes with 4 tablespoons water		
16 oz., Chunks		High for 10 to 12 minutes with 1/4 cup water, ice side up	Cover. Cook. Stir halfway through cooking time. Let stand, covered, 5 minutes.
CAULIFLOWER 1 lb. 14 oz. Whole, (1 medium head)	High for: 10 to 12 minutes		Rinse. Remove core in cone shape. Cover. Cook. Let stand, covered, 5 minutes.
1 lb. 3 oz., Flowerettes	7 to 8 minutes		Let stand, covered, 5 minutes.
10 oz., Flowerettes		High for 5 to 7 minutes with 1 tablespoon water, ice side up.	Let stand, covered, 3 minutes.
CELERY 4 cups, 1/4-inch slices	High for 6-1/2 to 7-1/2 minutes		Put in 2-qt. covered dish with water that clings from washing. Stir halfway through cooking time. Let stand, covered, 5 minutes.
CORN Whole, 1 ear, about 12-oz. 2 ears 4 ears 6 ears	High for: 2 to 3 minutes 3 to 5 minutes 7 to 8 minutes 9 to 10 minutes		Leave in closed husk. Wrap in wax paper or put in covered dish. Turn over halfway through cooking time. Let stand, covered, 5 minutes.
1 ear, about 9-oz. 2 ears 4 ears 6 ears		High for: 3-1/2 to 4 minutes 5 to 5-1/2 minutes 10 to 10-1/2 minutes 12 to 13 minutes	Wrap in wax paper. Turn over halfway through cooking time. Let stand, covered, 5 minutes.

Vegetable Cooking Table (Continued)

VEGETABLE	POWER SETTING AND APPROXIMATE TIMING		METHOD
	FRESH	FROZEN	
CORN, (Continued)			
Cut, 10 oz.		High for 5 to 6 minutes	Put in covered dish. Stir halfway through cooking time. Let stand, covered, 3 minutes.
EGGPLANT Cut into 1-inch cubes about 4 cups (1 medium)	High for 4-1/2 to 5-1/2 minutes		Peel with vegetable peeler. Cut into 1-inch cubes. Put in covered dish. Stir halfway through cooking time. Suggestion: Add butter, seasonings and Parmesan cheese after cooking.
MUSHROOMS 1 lb., Whole or sliced	High for 4 minutes		Wash and dry. Use 4-qt. covered dish. 1 to 2 tablespoons butter may be added before or during cooking. Stir twice.
OKRA 1 lb., Cut into 1/2-inch pieces	High for 5-1/2 to 6-1/2 minutes with 1 tablespoon water		Put in covered dish. Stir halfway through cooking time. Let stand, covered, 3 minutes.
ONIONS 1 lb., Whole (small)	High for 6 to 7 minutes		Put in covered dish. Stir halfway through cooking time. Let stand, covered, 3 to 5 minutes.
1 lb., Cut, into quarters	High for 5 to 6 minutes		
PARSNIPS 1 lb., Cut into quarters	High for 7 to 8 minutes with 1/4 cup water		Put in covered dish. Stir halfway through cooking time. Let stand, covered, 5 minutes.
PEAS, Shelled 1 lb., (1 cup)	High for: 3 minutes with 1 tablespoons water		
2 lbs., (2 cups)	5 minutes with 1-1/2 tablespoons water		Cook in covered dish. Stir halfway through cooking time. Let stand, covered, 3 minutes.
3 lbs., (3 cups)	6 minutes with 2 tablespoons water		
10 oz.		High for 5 to 6 minutes, ice side up	
PEAS AND CARROTS 10 oz., Cut		High for 6 to 7 minutes, ice side up	Cook in covered dish. Stir halfway. Let stand, covered, 3 minutes.
PEPPERS, green or red 1 lb. (about 2 large)	High for 6 to 7 minutes		Remove core; wash. Put in 2-qt. covered dish with water that clings from washing. Turn dish halfway through cooking time. Let stand 5 minutes.

Vegetable Cooking Table (Continued)

VEGETABLE	POWER SETTING AND APPROXIMATE TIMING		METHOD
	FRESH	FROZEN	
POTATOES, Baked, Whole, 7 oz. each	High for:		Pierce skins. Put on paper towel; allow 1-inch space between potatoes. Turn over halfway through cooking time. Let stand 10 minutes in Stay Hot or wrap in terry-cloth towel.
1 medium	4 to 4-1/2 minutes		
2 medium	7 to 7-1/2 minutes		
4 medium	11 to 12 minutes		
6 medium	17 to 18 minutes		
8 medium	22 to 23 minutes		
POTATOES, Boiled, 1-1/4 lb. Cut into halves or quarters, (about 3 medium)	High for 8 to 9 minutes		Cook with or without skins. Put in roasting bag or covered dish. Let stand 3 min-minutes, covered.
SPINACH Leaf, 1 lb. (about 2 bunches)	High for 5 to 7 minutes		Wash; put in 4-qt. covered casserole with water that clings to leaves from washing. Stir twice. Let stand, covered, 3 minutes.
Chopped, 10 oz. Leaf		High for 6 to 7 minutes, ice side up	Stir twice. Let stand, covered, 3 minutes.
SQUASH Acorn, 1-1/2 lbs. (1 medium) 3 lbs. (2 medium)	High for: 6 to 8 minutes 12 to 14 minutes		Pierce skin. Cook whole without covering. Let stand 5 minutes. Cut, seed and season.
Hubbard, 10 oz.		High for 5 to 6 minutes	Use 1-qt. covered casserole. Stir once. Let stand, covered, 3 to 5 minutes.
1 lb.	7 to 8 minutes		Put in covered dish. Turn dish halfway through cooking time. Let stand, covered, 5 minutes.
Zucchini, 1 lb. 1/2-inch slices	High for 8 to 10 minutes		Wash; put in covered dish with water that clings from washing. Stir once. Let stand, covered, 3 minutes.
TOMATOES 1-3/4 lbs., Whole (4 medium)	High for 4 to 5 minutes		Put in covered dish. Let stand, covered, 5 minutes. Puree if desired. Makes about 2 cups tomato sauce.
14 oz., Cut in half (2 medium)	High for 3 to 5 minutes		Put in plate or utility dish. Cover with wax paper. Let stand, covered, 3 minutes.
TURNIPS 1 lb., Diced (4 medium)	High for 6 to 8 minutes with 3 tablespoons water		Scrub. Dice. Put in covered dish. Stir halfway through cooking time. Let stand, covered, 5 minutes.

Weights shown are market-weight before trimming and cooking.

Sauces

A tasty sauce turns ordinary food into a superb delight. Sauces prepared in the microwave are simple and cook quickly. Try one. Pungent Barbecue Sauce will dress-up any meat. Creamy Hollandaise Sauce makes vegetables perfect. Boil flour or cornstarch-based sauces on High to cook thoroughly and thicken. Cook delicate egg-yolk sauces slowly on Low and don't boil.

You can cook sauce right in the measuring cup for easy stirring and pouring. Stir sauces halfway through cooking to eliminate lumps.

Sherried Meat Sauce

A spectacular moment in an elegant dinner.

8 to 10 fresh mushrooms, sliced
2 tablespoons chopped green onions
1 teaspoon lemon juice
1/4 teaspoon tarragon
1/4 teaspoon pepper
Drippings from beef roast or steak
2 tablespoons sherry

Add mushrooms, onions, lemon juice, tarragon and pepper to meat drippings. Cook on High for 2 minutes, stirring once. Pour hot sauce over meat. Warm sherry in a 1-cup glass measure or heat-resistant pitcher with handle on High for 30 seconds. Ignite with a match in the container for a spectacular serving finale. Be careful to hold your head away from the container opening when igniting.

Béchamel Sauce

A rich, white sauce to garnish chicken, seafood or vegetables.

1/4 cup butter or margarine
1/4 cup flour
1 cup chicken broth or bouillon

1 cup light cream
1/2 teaspoon salt
Dash of pepper and paprika

In 4-cup measure, melt butter on High for 40 seconds. Stir in flour. Cook on High for 1 minute, stirring once. Pour in broth, cream, salt, pepper and paprika. Cook on High for 3 minutes, stirring once every minute. Serve over chicken, seafood or vegetables. Makes about 2 cups of sauce.

Cheese Sauce

Makes every vegetable a success.

2 tablespoons butter
2 tablespoons flour
1/2 teaspoon salt

1 cup milk
1/2 cup grated sharp Cheddar cheese
Salt and pepper to taste

In 4-cup glass measure, melt butter on High for 30 seconds. Stir in flour and salt. Mix well. Add milk. Cook, uncovered, on High for 2 minutes, stirring after 1 minute. Add cheese and stir until well blended. Cook, uncovered, on High for 2 more minutes or until creamy, stirring twice. Salt and pepper to taste. Pour over hot vegetable. Makes 1-1/4 cups of sauce.

Hollandaise Sauce

Assured success—even for a beginner.

1/4 cup butter or margarine
1 tablespoon lemon juice,
    approximately 1/2 lemon
2 egg yolks, well beaten

1/4 cup light cream
1/2 teaspoon dry mustard
1/4 teaspoon salt

In 2-cup glass measure, melt butter or margarine on High for 40 seconds. Stir in lemon juice, then egg yolks and cream. Cook on High for 1 to 1-1/2 minutes, stirring every 15 to 30 seconds, Add seasonings. Beat until smooth. Makes 1 cup of sauce.

Clarified Butter

A connoisseur's delight!

1 cup butter (2 sticks)

In 2-cup liquid measure, melt butter slowly on Low for 1-1/2 to 2-1/2 minutes or until completely melted and oil starts to separate, but butter has not started to bubble or cook. Let butter stand a few minutes. Skim off foam. Slowly pour off yellow oil and reserve. This is the clarified butter. Discard leftover whey. Makes approximately 2/3 cup.

Béarnaise Sauce

Hollandaise sauce with tarragon flavor—fit for a broiled steak.

1/4 cup dry white wine
2 tablespoons white wine vinegar
1 tablespoon minced shallots
   or green onions
1 teaspoon dried tarragon, crushed

4 egg yolks, beaten
2/3 cup clarified butter
1/4 teaspoon salt
White pepper to taste
Dash cayenne

In 2-cup liquid measure, combine wine, vinegar, shallots or onions and tarragon. Bring to boil on High and continue cooking until about half of liquid is evaporated, 4 to 5 minutes. Strain liquid. Slowly pour hot strained liquid into egg yolks in a 1-1/2-quart casserole, beating constantly with a wire wisk. Cook on Low for 1 to 2 minutes, stirring with a wire wisk after 30 seconds, then every 15 seconds until sauce is consistency of mayonnaise. Gradually beat in clarified butter. Season with salt, pepper and cayenne. Cover and set dish in bowl of hot, not boiling, water to keep warm. Makes about 1 cup sauce.

Barbecue Sauce

A spicy blend for a special treat.

1 (8-oz.) can tomato sauce
1/4 cup vinegar
2 tablespoons brown sugar
1 teaspoon prepared mustard

1 tablespoon Worcestershire sauce
1 tablespoon instant minced onion
1/4 teaspoon salt
1/8 teaspoon liquid smoke

In 4-cup measure, combine all ingredients. Cover with plastic wrap. Cook on High for 5 minutes, stirring once. Let stand several minutes. Serve with ribs, chicken, chops, hamburger. Makes 1-1/4 cups.

Creole Sauce

Grated cheese provides the final touch.

1/2 cup chopped onion
1/4 cup chopped green pepper
1/4 cup chopped celery
2 tablespoons butter
1 fresh tomato, peeled and chopped

1 (8-oz.) can tomato sauce
1 (3-oz.) can mushrooms, not drained
1/4 teaspoon salt
1/8 teaspoon garlic powder

In 2-quart bowl, combine onion, pepper, celery and butter. Cover. Cook on High for 4 minutes. Stir in remaining ingredients. Cover. Cook on High for another 5 minutes. Serve over cooked fish or vegetables. Makes 2-1/2 cups of sauce.

Fresno Fruit Sauce

Sweet 'n fruity.

1/2 cup raisins
1/2 cup water
1/4 cup currant jelly
1/2 cup orange juice

1/4 cup brown sugar, firmly packed
1 tablespoon cornstarch
1/8 teaspoon allspice

In 4-cup measure, combine raisins with water, jelly and orange juice. Heat on High for 3 minutes or until jelly melts, stirring once. Mix sugar, cornstarch and allspice. Stir into raisin mixture. Cook on High for 1-1/2 minutes, stirring every 30 seconds. Serve with baked ham, pork chops or duck. Makes 1-1/2 cups of sauce.

Sweet-Sour Sauce

An intriguing combination of textures.

1/2 cup sugar
3 tablespoons cornstarch
1 cup chicken broth
1/2 cup vinegar

1/2 cup pineapple juice
2 teaspoons soy sauce
1/2 cup pineapple bits
1/2 green pepper, coarsely chopped

In 4-cup glass measure, blend sugar and cornstarch. Stir in the liquids. Cook on High for 8 minutes, stirring once or twice. Add pineapple bits and green pepper. Serve over meatballs. Makes about 2-1/2 cups of sauce.

From top in small pitcher: Fresno Fruit Sauce, Sweet-Sour Sauce, Creole Sauce.

Medium White Sauce

Make this during the meat and vegetable's standing time.

1/2 cup Basic Creamy-Sauce Mix, see below
1 cup water

In 4-cup measure, combine Basic Creamy-Sauce Mix and water. Cook on High for 4 minutes, stirring often. Use as sauce for chipped beef, cooked fish or vegetables. Makes 1 cup of sauce.

Basic Creamy-Sauce Mix

Make sauce in the microwave and eliminate lumps, burning and constant stirring.

This recipe is used to make Medium White Sauce, see above.

1-1/3 cups non-fat dried-milk powder
3/4 cup flour

1 teaspoon salt
1/2 cup butter or margarine

In mixing bowl, stir together milk powder, flour and salt. With pastry blender, cut in butter or margarine until mixture resembles small peas. Refrigerate in tightly covered container. Makes enough sauce for 6 cups Medium White Sauce.

Bordelaise Sauce

Make ahead and reheat as needed.

3 tablespoons butter or margarine
1 tablespoon minced onion
3 tablespoons flour
1 cup beef broth or bouillon
2 tablespoons red wine

1 tablespoon lemon juice
1/2 teaspoon dried tarragon, crushed
1 teaspoon finely chopped parsley
1/8 teaspoon brown sauce for gravy

In 4-cup measure, melt butter with onion for 1 minute on High. Stir in flour. Cook on High for 1 minute, stirring once. Pour in broth or bouillon, wine, lomon juice, tarragon and parsley. Cook on High for 3 minutes, stirring once every minute. Add brown sauce. Serve with broiled steak or roast beef. Makes 1-1/4 cups of sauce.

Butter-Crumb Topping

Make your own crumbs in the blender. Dry them in the microwave.

1/4 cup butter or margarine
1 cup bread crumbs, soft or dry

1/4 cup shredded Cheddar cheese (optional)

In 9-inch pie plate, melt butter or margarine on High for 40 seconds. Stir in bread crumbs and cheese, if desired. Cook on High for 1 minute. Sprinkle over cooked broccoli, green beans or stewed tomatoes. Makes 2 to 4 servings.

Browned Lemon Butter

So easy to prepare.

1/4 cup butter or margarine
1 tablespoon lemon juice

Dash Worcestershire sauce

In 9-inch pie plate, heat butter or margarine on top shelf with browning unit for 7 minutes or until it begins to turn golden. Cool slightly. Stir in lemon juice and Worcestershire sauce. Serve over cooked vegetables or fish. Makes 2 to 4 servings.

Gravy

Adds rich flavor every time.

1/2 cup drippings (fat and juices from meat)
1/2 cup flour
4 cups liquid (broth, juices or water)

Salt and pepper
Brown sauce for gravy (optional)

Pour drippings in 7-1/2" x 12" utility dish or 4-quart casserole. Stir in flour. Cook on High for 1 minute, stirring once. Pour in liquid, stirring until well blended. Cook on High 4 to 5 minutes or until thick, stirring several times. Season with salt and pepper. Add a few drops of brown sauce for a deeper brown color, if desired. Makes about 1 quart of gravy.

Tip *Refrigerate fresh-perked coffee. Reheat a cup at a time on High for 1-1/2 to 2 minutes.*

Convenience Foods

At one time or another we all use food that is pre-cooked or pre-mixed and packaged. Meals from a package are faster and more convenient than meals prepared from several separate ingredients.

Some convenience foods are frozen. You can buy frozen food in pouches, shallow foil trays or deep-dish foil trays. The method for thawing and heating differs according to the container. The object is to thaw and heat the food at the same time.

In general, defrost *cooked* foods on Medium and defrost *uncooked* foods on Low.

The timings given here are for a single food item.

If you heat 2 or more items simultaneously, increase the cooking time by about 1/2. For example, 1 item may heat in 6 minutes, but 2 heated together require only about 9 minutes.

To prepare convenience foods, check the tables and recipes in this section. Find the type of food and container that best resemble what you intend to cook. Follow the directions. Remember, it's better to undercook and then add another 15 to 30 seconds than to overcook.

These instructions concerning use of metal containers apply to Thermatronic ovens. If you have another brand, be sure to check the instructions that came with your oven.

Packaged Scalloped and Au Gratin Potatoes

Empty potato slices into a 3-quart casserole. Sprinkle with cheese-sauce mix. Add 2 tablespoons butter or margarine. Bring 2-1/4 cups water to boil on High for 5 to 6 minutes. Add 2/3 cup of milk. Pour over potato slices. Cook on High for 12 to 15 minutes, stirring twice. Raise shelf. Brown for 5 to 6 minutes.

Clockwise from top right: TV Dinner, Packaged Lasagna, Au Gratin Potatoes.

Instant Potatoes (for 4)

In 4-cup measure, put 1-1/3 cups water, 1/3 cup milk, 1/2 teaspoon salt and 2 tablespoons butter or margarine. Bring just to boiling on High for 4 to 5 minutes. Remove from oven. Stir in 1-1/3 cups instant potatoes and whip with fork to consistency desired. To make 8 to 12 servings, follow same procedure, using a larger, deep bowl for bringing water, milk and butter or margarine to a boil.

Skillet and Casserole Mixes

In 3-quart shallow casserole, cook 1 pound ground beef on High for 4 minutes. Stir often so meat will be crumbly, but stop cooking before all pinkness is gone from meat. Add the remaining packaged ingredients and water. Cover. Cook on High for 8 minutes. Stir after 4 minutes and 6 minutes of cooking time. Let stand, covered, for 5 minutes.

Stuffing Mixes

Use instructions on the box. Place water, butter or margarine and seasoning mix in a 2-quart casserole. Cover. Bring to a boil on High. Add stuffing mix and stir. Let stand, covered, for 5 minutes. Before serving, reheat on High for 1 minute.

Rice Mixes

In 4-quart casserole, put 1-3/4 to 2 cups of water, 2 tablespoons butter or margarine and contents of the seasoning envelope. Bring to a boil on High for 4 to 5 minutes. Add rice and stir well. Cover. Cook on High for 8 to 10 minutes. Stir and leave covered for 5 to 10 minutes. Fluff with fork at serving time.

Pasta

Egg noodles (4 cups), or macaroni (2 cups), or spaghetti (7-oz.)
2-1/2 cups water

In a 4-quart covered casserole, bring water to boil, approximately 5 to 8 minutes on High. Add pasta, salt and 1 teaspoon oil to boiling water. Cook, uncovered, 5 to 7 minutes on High, stirring once. Let stand covered 5 to 10 minutes. Drain thoroughly.

Tip   *Soften hard ice cream for easier serving. Warm on High for 10 to 15 seconds. Let stand 2 to 3 minutes. Repeat for 5 seconds, if necessary.*

Frozen Convenience Foods in Pouches

It's possible to cook successfully in the pouch. However, it's difficult to remove hot food from a pouch with slits. Put the pouch in a covered dish that conforms to the size of the food. Then make several slits in the pouch to let steam escape. Otherwise follow the directions below.

FOOD	DIRECTIONS
11-oz. Creamed Chipped Beef	Remove from pouch. Heat on Medium for 3 minutes. Stir. Heat on Medium for 3 more minutes.
10-1/2-oz. Green-Pepper Steak with Rice	Heat rice in pouch and steak in covered dish together on Medium for 6 minutes.
10-oz. Beef Stew	Remove from pouch. Heat on Medium for 7 minutes. Stir halfway through cooking time.
12-oz. Chow Mein	Remove from pouch. Heat on Medium for 6 minutes. Stir. Heat on Medium for 2 minutes. Let stand for 2 to 3 minutes.
14-oz. Spaghetti with Meat Sauce	Leave spaghetti in pouch. Slit bag and put sauce in covered dish. Heat on Medium for 4 minutes. Stir. Heat on Medium for 3 minutes.

To cook vegetables in pouches, cut an "X" slit in the bag so steam can escape.

Frozen Convenience Foods in Shallow Foil Trays

The foil tray should be 7/8-inch deep or less. Peel off the foil cover and slip tray back into the box* unless otherwise indicated. Allow food to stand at least 2 minutes after thawing and heating.

FOOD	DIRECTIONS
4-1/2-oz. French Toast with Link Sausages	With wax paper over tray, heat on Medium for 2 minutes. Turn toast over. Heat on Medium for 1/2 to 1 minute.
12 (5-1/2-oz.) Cocktail Tacos	Place on rack in utility dish on upper shelf. Heat on High for 2-1/2 minutes. Separate tacos. Crisp on Stay Hot for 10 minutes.
12 Egg Rolls	Place on rack in utility dish on upper shelf. Heat on High for 2-3/4 minutes. Crisp on Stay Hot.
11-1/2-oz. Roast Beef Hash	Heat on Medium for 9 to 11 minutes. Stir halfway through cooking time. Brown.
7-1/2-oz. Enchilada	Heat on Medium for 7 to 9 minutes. Turn over halfway through cooking time.
11-1/2-oz. Chicken Dinner	Keep dessert only covered with foil until halfway through cooking time. Remove foil and slip dinner back into box. Heat on Medium for 10 minutes.
12-oz. Enchilada Dinner	Remove foil and slip dinner back in box. Heat on Medium for 9 minutes.
13-oz. Polynesian-Style Dinner	Cover dessert with foil. Heat on Medium for 8 minutes. Remove foil. Heat in box on Medium for 4 minutes.
20-oz. Veal-Parmesan Dinner	Cover dessert with foil. Heat on Medium for 12 minutes. Remove foil. Heat in box on Medium for 6 minutes.
10-oz. Meat Pie, single-crust	Place shelf in upper position. Heat on Medium for 10 to 12 minutes or until crust appears cooked. Turn twice during heating. Remove from package. Brown 3 to 4 minutes.

*If foil tray is loosely covered with plastic wrap, place paper towel under foil tray to protect shelf from arcing.

Frozen Convenience Foods in Deep-Dish Foil Trays

These metal-type trays are so deep that the microwaves can't reach the food to cook it thoroughly. Remove the food from the foil tray and put it in a covered dish that most nearly conforms to the shape and size of the food. Because the ice crystals in the center of foods are slowest to thaw, stir or rearrange the food halfway through the cooking time.

FOOD	DIRECTIONS
12-oz. Noodles Romanoff	Remove from foil tray and put in a covered dish. Heat on Medium for 8 to 9 minutes. Stir halfway through cooking time. Let stand 3 to 5 minutes.
12-oz. Macaroni and Cheese	Remove from foil tray and put in a covered dish. Heat on Low for 14 minutes. Stir halfway through cooking time. Brown 3 to 5 minutes.
11-oz. Spaghetti with Meat Sauce	Heat on Medium for 10 minutes. Stir halfway through cooking time.
11-1/2-oz. Tuna Noodle Casserole	Remove from foil tray and put in a covered dish. Heat on Medium for 8 to 9 minutes. Stir halfway through cooking time. Let stand 3 to 5 minutes.
21-oz. Lasagna with Meat Sauce	Remove from foil tray and put in a covered dish. Heat on Low for 25 minutes. Halfway through cooking time cut in half; turn center of food to outside of dish.
16-3/4-oz. Stuffed Shells, Beef and Spinach	Remove from foil tray and put in a covered dish. Heat on Low for 20 minutes. Separate halfway through cooking time; turn center of food to outside of dish.
14-oz. Stuffed Green Peppers	Remove from foil tray and put in a covered dish. Heat on Medium for 10 minutes. Break peppers apart. Heat on Medium for 5 minutes.
14-oz. Stuffed Cabbage Rolls	Remove from foil tray and put in a covered dish. Heat on Medium for 12 minutes. Stir or turn halfway through cooking time. Let stand for 5 minutes.
11-1/2-oz. Roast-Beef Hash	Remove from foil tray and put in a covered dish. Heat on Medium for 8 to 9 minutes. Stir halfway through cooking time.
8-1/2-oz. Chicken Divan	Remove from foil tray and put in a covered dish. Heat on Medium for 4 minutes. Turn. Heat on Medium for 4 to 5 minutes.
2-lbs. Fried Chicken	Put chicken on rack in utility dish and place on upper shelf. Heat, uncovered, on Medium for 6 minutes. Crisp with Browner or Stay Hot.
1-lb. Fish Kabobs	Put kabobs on rack in utility dish. Place shelf in upper position. Heat, uncovered, on Medium for 6 minutes. Crisp with Browner or Stay Hot.
1-lb. Breaded Fish Sticks or Patties	Follow same procedure used for Fish Kabobs.

135

Frozen Convenience Foods in Deep-Dish Foil Trays (Continued)

FOOD	DIRECTIONS
16-oz. Baked Beans	Remove from foil tray and put in a covered dish. Heat on Medium for 8-1/2 minutes. Stir halfway through cooking time. Let stand, covered, for 3 minutes.
12-oz. Stuffed Baked Potatoes	Remove from foil tray and put in a covered dish. Heat on Medium for 8-1/2 to 9-1/2 minutes. Halfway through cooking time separate; turn center of food to outside of dish. Let stand, covered, for 3 to 5 minutes.
1-lb. Tater Tots®	Put potatoes on rack in utility dish. Place shelf in upper position. Heat, uncovered, on Medium for 8 minutes. Turn halfway through cooking time. Crisp with Stay Hot or Browner.
12-oz. Vegetable Soufflé	Remove from foil tray and put in a covered dish. Heat on Medium for 6 minutes. Stir. Heat on Medium for 6 minutes more. Stir if center is still soft. Let stand 3 to 5 minutes.
10-oz. Vegetable au Gratin	Remove from foil tray and put in a covered dish. Heat on Medium for 4 minutes. Break apart in center. Heat on Medium for 4 minutes more. Let stand 2 minutes.
16-oz. Meat Pie, single crust	Leave in foil tray. Make knife slits through crust. Place shelf in upper position. Heat on Medium for 7 minutes. Turn. Heat for 7 minutes more or until crust appears cooked. Brown 2-1/2 to 3 minutes.
32-oz. Barbecue Sauce with Sliced Beef	Heat on Medium 2 minutes to loosen from container. Remove from foil tray and put in covered dish. Heat on Medium for 6 minutes. Break apart in center. Heat on Medium for 6 minutes more. Let stand 3 to 5 minutes.

To heat fresh tortillas, wrap 1 to 12 in a cloth towel or napkin. Heat on High for 1 to 2 minutes. Tortillas will stay soft and warm if left covered. Heat crepes the same way.

Eggs & Cheese

Eggs and cheese are delicious, delicate foods that cook quickly in a microwave oven. Heating them too fast or too long makes them tough. Give eggs close attention while they cook. Stir them often or turn the dish and keep a watchful eye on them during the last stages of cooking.

Use care when you cook eggs individually. The yolk, which is mainly fat, cooks faster than the white, which is mainly water. This problem is reduced by mixing the yolk and the white together, as in scrambled eggs, or surrounding the egg by a liquid, as in poached eggs.

Don't try to hard-cook eggs in your microwave oven, even though they are in water. **Always remove the shells before cooking eggs in your microwave** or they may explode.

You can "fry" an egg in a browning dish. Check the instructions that come with your browning dish. Without a browning dish, the closest method to frying is a "froached" egg—a combination of fried and poached—See Egg Cooking Table, page 143.

Cheese stirred into a casserole reacts slower to heat than cheese laid on the top. If you use cheese as a topping, add it during the last 2 minutes of cooking.

See Egg Cooking Table, page 143.

Eggs Benedict

Vinegar in the water helps set the egg white.

4 halves toasted English muffins
4 slices cooked ham
2 cups water

1 teaspoon vinegar
4 eggs
Hollandaise Sauce, page 124

Arrange muffin halves in 7-1/2" x 12" utility dish. Top with ham. To poach eggs, place 2 cups of hot water in 2-quart covered casserole, cover and bring to a boil on High. Pierce the egg yolks with a toothpick or fork. Add vinegar and swirl water with spoon. Carefully slip eggs, one at a time, into the water. Cover. Cook on Low for 2 minutes. Remove eggs with slotted spoon and arrange 1 poached egg on each ham slice. Spoon Hollandaise Sauce over all. Cook on High for about 1 minute or until heated. Makes 4 servings.

Cheese Soufflé

Serve this delectable dish with confidence.

Sauce:

1/4 cup all-purpose flour
3/4 teaspoon dry mustard
3/4 teaspoon salt
1/4 teaspoon paprika

1/8 teaspoon cayenne pepper
1 (13-oz.) can evaporated milk
2 cups lightly packed, grated sharp
   Cheddar cheese

Soufflé:

6 eggs, separated
1 teaspoon cream of tartar

Sauce:

In 4-cup measure, add flour, dry mustard, salt, paprika and cayenne pepper. Slowly add evaporated milk and mix together until smooth. Cook on High for 3 or 4 minutes or until sauce thickens. Stir after 2 minutes, then every 30 seconds. Add cheese and mix until cheese is melted. Set aside.

Soufflé:

In large mixing bowl, beat egg whites and cream of tartar with electric mixer until stiff, but not dry. In a medium bowl, beat egg yolks until thick and lemon-colored. Gradually add cheese sauce to egg yolks until thoroughly blended. Fold mixture carefully into beaten egg whites. Put into ungreased 2-quart soufflé dish. Cook on Low for 18 to 20 minutes or until top is dry, giving dish a quarter turn every 5 minutes. Serve immediately. Makes 6 servings.

Tip   *For foods with a smooth and even texture, stir at least once to bring the outside cooking portions to the center and the less-cooked portions to the outside.*

Tijuana Quiche

A luncheon treat from the Southwest.

2 cups shredded Monterey Jack cheese
1 cup shredded Cheddar cheese
Pastry for One-Crust Pie, page 161
1 (4-oz.) can green chiles, chopped;
   discard seeds and pits
1 cup half and half, room temperature

1/4 teaspoon salt
1/8 teaspoon ground cumin
3 eggs, slightly beaten,
   room temperature

Sprinkle half the Cheddar and all the Jack cheese over the bottom of the baked pie crust, distributing the chiles throughout. Save 2 tablespoons of the chiles and set aside with half the Cheddar cheese. In a 4-cup measure, heat half and half with salt and cumin on High for 2-1/2 to 3 minutes, stirring occasionally. It will thicken slightly. Do not let boil. Slowly stir half and half into eggs. Pour mixture into pie crust. Sprinkle remaining Cheddar cheese and chiles lightly over pie filling. Raise shelf. Cook on Low for 10 minutes, turning once. Brown 4 to 5 minutes, turning once. Serve hot or cold. Makes 6 servings.

Crab Quiche

A delicious experience.

6 oz. frozen crab or lobster
1 tablespoon sherry
1 cup half and half
1 tablespoon butter
1 tablespoon instant minced onion
1 teaspoon salt

1/4 teaspoon ground white pepper
4 eggs, beaten
2 cups grated Swiss cheese
Pastry for One-Crust Pie, page 161
1 tablespoon sherry

Thaw frozen crab or lobster on Low for 2-1/2 minutes. Let stand. Drain. Add 1 tablespoon sherry to crab or lobster and set aside. In a 4-cup glass measuring cup, heat the half and half, butter, onion, salt and pepper on High for 3 minutes. Add slowly to beaten eggs. Sprinkle the cheese over the baked crust, reserving 1/4 cup for the topping. Add the crab or lobster with the sherry in which it has been marinated. Pour in the cream-and-egg mixture. Top with remaining cheese and 1 tablespoon sherry. Raise shelf. Cook on Low for 10 minutes, turning plate twice. Brown 4 to 5 minutes. Makes 8 servings.

 *Tip*   *For a quick breakfast, heat 2 refrigerated pancakes on High for 35 to 40 seconds. Heat 2 refrigerated waffles on High for 25 to 30 seconds.*

..iche Lorraine

..elegant brunch or supper.

6 slices bacon	Dash cayenne pepper
1 cup grated Swiss cheese	1-1/2 tablespoons flour
Pastry for One-Crust Pie, page 161	1 (13-oz.) can evaporated milk
1/4 teaspoon salt	4 eggs, slightly beaten
1/4 teaspoon nutmeg	3 green onions, thinly sliced

Place bacon on metal rack in the utility dish. Cover with paper towel. Cook on High for 6 minutes; crumble into small pieces. Sprinkle 1/2 of bacon and all of cheese over baked crust. In a 4-cup measure, mix salt, nutmeg, cayenne and flour. Gradually stir in milk, blending well. Cook on High for 3-1/2 minutes or until bubbly, stirring twice. Slowly stir hot creamy mixture into eggs. Pour over bacon and cheese in pie crust. Top with remaining bacon and green onions. Raise shelf. Cook on Low for 10 minutes. Brown 5 minutes, turning once. Makes 6 servings.

Poached Eggs

Start the day with a nutritious breakfast.

2 cups water	2 eggs
1 teaspoon vinegar	

In 1-quart casserole, bring water to boil on High. Add vinegar. Swirl the water with a spoon. Add the eggs and cover. Cook on Low for 1 minute. Remove eggs with slotted spoon. Makes 2 poached eggs.

Quiche Lorraine

Tip *Warm honey, corn syrup or maple syrup in serving pitcher—glass or earthenware—on High for 30 to 45 seconds.*

Creamy Scrambled Eggs

Something wonderful happens with this cheese-and-egg combination.

6 eggs
1/4 cup milk
1/4 teaspoon salt
Dash pepper

2 tablespoons butter or margarine
1 (3-oz.) pkg. cream cheese,
   cut in 1/2-inch cubes
Chopped chives

Mix eggs with milk, salt and pepper. In 2-quart casserole, melt butter or margarine on High for 30 seconds. Pour in egg mixture. Cook on Low for 6 minutes, stirring occasionally the last 3 minutes of cooking. Add cream-cheese cubes. Cook on Low for 45 to 60 seconds. Sprinkle with chives. Makes 4 servings.

Corn Pudding

A new look for some old favorites.

One bunch green onions, chopped
1/4 cup chopped green pepper
4 to 6 tablespoons butter
3 eggs, beaten
5 cups canned corn, drained, or kernels
   from 5 or 6 ears fresh corn

3/4 cup mocha mix
3 tablespoons sugar
2 tablespoons flour
1/2 teaspoon salt

In 2-quart covered casserole, partially cook onions, green pepper and butter on High for 3 minutes. Mix the remaining ingredients together and add to the onion-green-pepper mixture. Stir. Cover. Cook on Low for 20 minutes, turning dish a half turn after 10 minutes. Remove cover. Raise shelf. Brown 5 to 6 minutes. Makes 6 to 8 servings.

 *Tip* — *To liquify honey that has turned to sugar, heat on High for 30 to 45 seconds.*

Egg Cooking Table

This table is only a guide. Cooking times will vary with size, temperature and number of eggs cooked at one time.

TYPE	NUMBER	DIRECTIONS
Froached	1	In dish melt 1 teaspoon of butter on High for 30 seconds. Add egg. Cover. Cook on Low for 1-1/4 to 1-3/4 minutes. Let stand, covered, for 3 minutes.
	2	Cook in a 10-ounce custard cup, covered loosely with plastic wrap, on Low for 2-1/2 to 3 minutes. Let stand, covered, for 3 minutes.
Poached	1	Boil 1 cup water, covered, on High for about 2 to 3 minutes. Add egg. Cook, uncovered, on Low for 1 to 1-1/2 minutes.
	2	Cook, uncovered, on Low for 1-1/2 to 2 minutes.
Scrambled	1	Cook with 1 teaspoon water and butter on Low for 1-1/2 to 2 minutes.
	2	Cook with 1 teaspoon water and 1 teaspoon butter for each egg on Low for 2-1/2 to 3 minutes.
	4	Cook with 1 teaspoon water and butter for each egg on High for 2-1/2 to 3 minutes. STIR EVERY 30 TO 45 SECONDS WHEN USING HIGH.
Soft-Cooked		Similar to froached-egg procedure. Chop while soft.

DO NOT COOK EGGS IN THE SHELL—THEY MAY EXPLODE!

Breads & Cereals

Now there's no excuse for not having hot, fresh-from-the-oven bread, rolls or muffins. In a microwave oven, bread preparation can be done in a fraction of the time. You can bake your own bread, including some kinds of yeast breads, freeze it and use your microwave again to defrost it. Store-bought bread tastes fresh-baked when you warm it in your microwave. Better still, dress-up a loaf of French bread following the recipe for Hot French Herb-Bread. Make your own Sour Cream Coffee Cake. Quick breads are still quicker in the microwave. See the Quick Breads Table, page 152.

Bread cooks and reheats rapidly. Overheating makes it tough. Keep bread at serving temperature without overheating by using the Stay Hot. Place a paper napkin or paper towel under bread to prevent a soggy bottom.

Hot cereal from the microwave will be ready in just a few minutes. For a special breakfast or snack treat try Make-Your-Own Toasted Cereal.

See Quick Breads Table and Warming Baked-Breads Table, page 152.

Whole-Wheat Banana Bread

Full of hearty, moist flavor.

1/2 cup butter or margarine	1 cup whole-wheat flour
1 cup sugar	1 teaspoon soda
2 eggs, slightly beaten	1/2 teaspoon salt
1 cup (about 3 medium) mashed bananas	1/3 cup hot water
1 cup white, all-purpose flour	1/2 cup chopped walnuts

Melt butter or margarine on High for 45 seconds. Blend in sugar. Mix with beaten eggs and bananas until smooth. Sift white flour; measure. Sift again with whole-wheat flour, soda and salt. Add dry ingredients to banana mixture alternately with hot water. Stir in nuts. Line 9" x 5" loaf dish with wax paper. Pour batter into dish. Cook on Medium for 18 to 19 minutes, giving dish a quarter turn 3 times. Brown 4 to 5 minutes. Let cool for 10 minutes. Remove from dish and cool completely. Makes 1 loaf.

Pilgrim's Pumpkin Bread

Substitute this cake-like bread for a sweet dessert.

1-1/2 cups sugar
1-1/2 cups flour
1 teaspoon salt
1 teaspoon soda
1 teaspoon cinnamon
1/2 teaspoon nutmeg
1/4 teaspoon cloves

1/2 cup salad oil
1/3 cup water
2 eggs
1 cup canned pumpkin
1/2 cup chopped walnuts
1/2 cup chopped pitted dates

In large mixing bowl, combine all dry ingredients. Using an electric mixer, add the oil, water, eggs and pumpkin. Mix only until thoroughly blended, about 1 minute. Fold the nuts and dates into the batter. Pour into a greased 10-cup ring mold that has been sprinkled with cinnamon. Cook on Medium for 13 to 15 minutes, turning twice. If you do not have a plastic or ceramic 10-cup ring mold or Bundt dish, divide the batter in half and bake in a greased 1-1/2-quart loaf dish. Cool 10 minutes. Turn out of dish. Makes 2 loaves.

Date-Nut Bread

Serve with a salad for a tasty, light supper.

3/4 cup water
3/4 cup finely chopped dates
2 tablespoons shortening
1 egg
1-1/4 cups flour
1/4 cup brown sugar, firmly packed

1/2 teaspoon soda
1/2 teaspoon salt
1/2 teaspoon cinnamon
1/4 teaspoon nutmeg
1/2 cup chopped nuts

Heat water to boiling and pour over dates. Stir to break dates apart. Add shortening so it will melt. Let cool to room temperature. Beat egg and add to date mixture. Sift dry ingredients together. Add date mixture to dry ingredients, stirring only until mixed. Stir in nuts. Pour into greased 8-3/4" x 5-1/4" x 2-1/4" loaf dish. Bake on Medium for 7-1/2 to 8-1/2 minutes. Give dish a half turn after 4 minutes. Bread is done when toothpick inserted in center comes out clean. Allow to cool 10 minutes before removing from dish to cooling rack. Makes 1 loaf.

Tip *Toast shelled nuts or dried seeds on High in a single layer on a shallow paper or glass plate. Allow about 3 to 6 minutes per cupful. Stir twice. Season as you like.*

Chili-Cheese Corn Bread

A meal in itself.

2 eggs
1 cup sour cream
1 (8-oz.) pkg. corn-bread mix

1 (8-oz.) can whole-kernel corn, drained
1 (4-oz.) can diced green chiles, drained
1 cup grated Monterey Jack cheese

Grease an 8-1/2-inch ceramic ring mold. Blend eggs, sour cream and mix. Stir in drained corn. Pour half the batter into ring mold. Sprinkle on chiles and half the cheese. Pour on remaining batter and top with cheese. Cover with plastic wrap. Raise shelf. Bake on Medium for 5 minutes. Turn dish and remove plastic wrap. Cook on Medium for 4 to 5 minutes. Brown 4 minutes. Makes 9 servings.

Sally Lunn Dill Bread

Serve with hearty soup for a marvelous duo.

1 pkg. dry yeast
1/2 cup warm water (110°F, 43°C)
1 cup large-curd or small-curd cottage cheese
2 tablespoons sugar
1 tablespoon instant minced onion
1 tablespoon butter

2 teaspoons dill seed
1 teaspoon garlic salt
1/4 teaspoon soda
1 unbeaten egg
2-1/2 cups flour, sifted

Soften yeast in warm water. Heat cottage cheese to lukewarm on Low for 2 minutes. Combine all the ingredients except flour, beating with a mixer; gradually add flour. Cover. Let rise in warm place until doubled in size—about 50 minutes. Stir down with spoon. Turn into well-greased 8-inch round bowl. Let rise until dough just reaches the top of the bowl. Brown 7 minutes. Cook on Low for 8 to 9 minutes. Give dish a quarter turn halfway through cooking time. Brush top with butter. Let stand on counter top in the dish for 5 minutes. Turn out of dish and brown bottom if desired. Makes 1 loaf.

Dill-Cheese Loaf

The tempting aroma will draw a crowd.

2 cups pancake mix
1 tablespoon sugar
1 tablespoon instant minced onion
1 teaspoon dill weed
1 cup buttermilk or sour milk

1 egg
1 tablespoon melted butter or
   margarine
1 cup grated Swiss or
   Monterey Jack cheese

Line bottom of 8" x 4" loaf-shaped baking dish with wax paper. In mixing bowl, combine all ingredients except cheese. Blend with mixer on low speed; beat 2 minutes on medium speed. Stir in cheese. Pour into baking dish. Raise shelf. Cook on High for 8 minutes. Give dish a quarter turn every 2 minutes. Brown 4 minutes. Let stand 5 minutes before serving. Makes 1 loaf.

Caramel Biscuit Ring

Delicious with coffee or cocoa.

1/3 cup brown sugar, firmly packed
3 tablespoons butter
1 tablespoon water

1/2 teaspoon cinnamon
1/3 cup chopped nuts
1 (8-oz.) can refrigerator biscuits

In 8-inch round cake dish, combine brown sugar, butter, water and cinnamon. Cook on High for 1 minute. When butter is melted, stir in nuts. Separate can of biscuits into ten and cut each into quarters. Add to sugar mixture and stir to coat each piece. Push biscuits away from center and set a custard cup or glass in center. Cook on High for 2-1/2 to 3 minutes. Remove custard cup. Raise shelf. Brown 5 minutes. Pull sections apart and serve warm. Makes one 9-inch ring.

Packaged Nut-Bread Mix

A quick and easy complement for any meal.

1 (1-lb., 1-oz.) pkg. nut-bread mix
1 cup water

1 egg

Make batter as directed on package. Pour batter into a greased 8-1/2" x 4-1/2" x 2-1/2" loaf dish. Bake on Low for 14 to 16 minutes. Give dish a half turn halfway through cooking time. Brown for 5 minutes. Let stand 10 minutes before turning out on cooling rack. Makes 1 loaf.

Bill's Bran Muffins

Hot, homemade muffins for your family every morning.

4 eggs	5 teaspoons soda
1 quart buttermilk	2 teaspoons salt
5 cups flour	1 cup oil
3 cups sugar	1 (15-oz.) box raisin bran

In large bowl, beat eggs and blend with buttermilk. Add flour, sugar, soda and salt. Mix in oil and bran flakes. Allow batter to set for 24 hours. Keep covered in refrigerator up to 6 weeks. Spoon out muffins as needed. Cook in plastic cupcake utensil or custard cups, filling cups half full of batter. If custard cups are used, place cups in a circle on a large plate. Because batter is cold, timings are slightly longer than usual.

To make 2 muffins:	Cook on Medium for 2 to 2-1/2 minutes.
To make 4 muffins:	Cook on Medium for 2-1/2 to 3-1/2 minutes.
To make 6 muffins:	Cook on Medium for 3-1/2 to 4-1/2 minutes.

Remove muffins from utensil immediately after baking to cool. Makes 6 to 8 dozen muffins.

Hot French Herb Bread

A few minutes under the Stay Hot gives a crunchy, crisp crust.

1/2 loaf unsliced French bread	1 tablespoon Italian-herb seasoning
1/2 cup soft butter or margarine	Grated Parmesan cheese

Cut bread into 6 thick slices, being careful not to cut through bottom crust. Combine butter or margarine with seasonings. Spread between bread slices. Sprinkle cheese on top. Cook on Low for 1-1/2 to 2 minutes or until hot. Serve immediately or use Stay Hot for 10 minutes to crisp. Makes 6 servings.

Bill's Bran Muffins

Tip   *Dry 1/2 cup fresh herbs between paper towels on High for 2 minutes or until dried.*

Sour-Cream Coffee Cake

Make enough for a party or freeze the extra one.

1/2 cup butter or margarine
1 cup sugar
3 eggs
1 teaspoon vanilla
1-1/2 cups cake flour

1/2 cup all-purpose flour
1 teaspoon baking powder
1 teaspoon baking soda
1/2 pint dairy sour cream

Topping:
3/4 cup brown sugar, firmly packed
1/3 cup soft butter or margarine
4 tablespoons flour

1/4 teaspoon salt
1/4 teaspoon cinnamon
1/4 cup chopped nuts

Cream butter or margarine and sugar together. Beat in eggs. Add vanilla. Sift together flours, baking powder and baking soda. Fold in flour mixture and sour cream alternately. Flour mixture should be added first and last. Line the bottom of two 8-1/4-inch baking dishes with 2 layers of wax paper. Place 1/4 of the batter in each cake dish. Sprinkle each cake with 1/4 of the topping. Using icing knife, spread the remainder of the batter over each cake. Sprinkle with remaining topping. Bake each layer on Medium for 8 minutes. Brown 4 to 5 minutes. Let cakes cool in dishes before turning onto cooling rack. Makes two 8-1/4-inch coffee cakes.

Topping:
Cut brown sugar, butter or margarine, flour, salt and cinnamon together with pastry blender. Add nuts.

Variation:
If you are in a hurry, use a packaged yellow-cake mix and the above topping. Remember, you can freeze the second cooked coffee cake and defrost it on Low in 1-1/2 minutes.

Microwave Rice

Make plenty and use it with leftovers.

2 cups water
1 cup uncooked long-grain rice
1/2 teaspoon salt

Place water in 2-1/2-quart casserole. Bring to boil on High for 3-1/2 to 4 minutes. Add rice and salt. Stir and cover. Cook on High for 10 minutes. Let stand 10 minutes before serving. Makes 4 to 6 servings.

Oatmeal

So easy a child can fix it.

1 cup water
1/3 cup oatmeal

In 1-1/2-quart covered casserole, bring water to a boil on High for 2-1/2 to 3 minutes. Stir in oats. Cook, uncovered, on High for 1 minute. Stir. Cook, uncovered, on Low for 2 minutes. Let stand a few minutes before serving. Makes 1 serving.

Cream of Wheat®

No hard-to-wash pan when you cook it in the microwave.

1 cup water
2-1/2 tablespoons Cream of Wheat®

In 1-1/2-quart covered casserole, bring water to a boil on High for 2-1/2 to 3 minutes. Add cereal; stir well. Cook, uncovered, on High for 1 minute. Stir and cover. Cook on Low for 2 minutes. Let stand a few minutes before serving. Makes 1 serving.

Make-Your-Own Toasted Cereal

Tasty snackin', too.

1/3 cup chopped blanched almonds
1 cup quick-cooking rolled oats
1/3 cup wheat germ

1/3 cup raisins
1/3 cup chopped dried apples or apricots
1/4 cup brown sugar, firmly packed

Combine almonds, rolled oats and wheat germ. Spread in 7-1/2" x 12" utility dish. Raise shelf. Brown for 10 minutes, stirring occasionally. Remove from heat. Stir in raisins, apples or apricots and brown sugar. Store in refrigerator. Serve with milk or cream. Makes about 2-1/2 cups.

Variation:
Triple the recipe and store in refrigerator. For a crisper cereal, use the Stay Hot with the shelf in its lower position.

Quick Breads Table

	UTENSIL	TIME AND POWER LEVEL
Corn Bread Mix (8-oz.)	8-inch square dish	Medium for 6-1/2 to 7-1/2 minutes. Raise shelf and brown.
Corn Muffin Mix (6-oz.)	plastic cupcake utensil or custard cups	Medium for 2-1/2 minutes. Remove from utensil or cups immediately after cooking to cool.
Bran Muffin Mix (6-oz.)	plastic cupcake utensils or custard cups	Medium for 3-1/2 minutes. Remove from utensil or cups immediately after cooking to cool.
Quick Bread Mix (1-lb., 1-oz.)	8-1/2"x4-1/2"x2-1/2" loaf dish	Low for 14 to 16 minutes.
Coffee Cake Mix (13-oz.)	8-inch round cake dish	Medium for 8 to 9 minutes. Raise shelf and brown.

Warming Baked-Breads Table

Heat until just warm to touch. The inside will then always be hot.

VARIETY	AMOUNT	TIME AND POWER LEVEL
Buns Hamburger or	2	Low for: 30 seconds.
Hot Dog	6	1-1/4 minutes. After warming, cover and use Stay Hot.
French Bread, sliced	1/2 loaf, (8-oz.)	Low for 1-1/4 minutes. Use Stay Hot to crisp crust.
Muffins	1 2 3	Low for: 10 to 15 seconds 15 to 20 seconds 25 to 30 seconds
Rolls Dinner	12	Low for 1-1/2 to 2 minutes.
Sweet, with glaze	6	Low for 1 minute. After warming, cover and use Stay Hot.

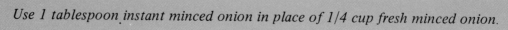
Tip *Use 1 tablespoon instant minced onion in place of 1/4 cup fresh minced onion.*

Calorie Counters

Thoughtful cooks always have a few favorite low-calorie recipes to make life pleasant for dieters. The recipes here are high in flavor and low in calories. Try spicy Meatball Soup or tender Italian Chicken smothered in onions and mushrooms. For a festive low-calorie meal with a Chinese touch, try Shrimp Sauté with Bean Sprouts. Another treat with calories left out is Chicken Surprise, a hearty tomato-chicken combination.

Dieters will enjoy these taste-tempting flavors and they'll never miss the calories.

Italian Chicken

A savory blend of onions and mushrooms dresses up tender chicken.

1-1/2 lbs. chicken breasts, boned,
  skinned and halved
1/4 cup salad oil
1 garlic clove, minced

1 medium onion, thinly sliced
  separated into rings
1 (8-oz.) can chicken consommé
1/2 lb. fresh mushrooms, sliced

Cut breasts into quarters. Remove skin. Preheat browning dish on High for 7 minutes. Add oil, garlic and chicken pieces, meaty side down. Cook on Medium for 3 minutes. Turn chicken over. Cook on Medium for 3 minutes more. Remove chicken from dish and set aside. Add onions and consommé to dish. Cook on High for 3 minutes. Add chicken and cover dish. Cook on Medium for 15 minutes. Add mushrooms and cover. Cook on Medium for 5 minutes. Makes 3 servings.

Chicken Cacciatora

A delicious dish that's low in calories, too!

2 lbs. chicken breasts
Seasoned salt
1 to 1-1/2 cups sliced mushrooms
2 cups stewed tomatoes
2 small green peppers, chopped
2 tablespoons finely chopped pimiento

3 teaspoons dried parsley
1 teaspoon salt
1/4 teaspoon dried thyme
1 clove garlic, pressed
1 bay leaf
Pepper to taste

Place chicken pieces in a 7-1/2" x 12" utility dish. Sprinkle lightly with seasoned salt and top with mushrooms. In a 4-cup measure, combine remaining ingredients. Cook on High for 5 minutes or until mixture comes to a boil. Pour over chicken and mushrooms. Cover. Cook on Medium for 20 minutes. Makes 4 servings.

Chicken Surprise

Tender chicken, spicy sauce and a minimum of calories.

2 lbs. chicken breasts, skinned and halved
1 garlic clove, minced

1/2 teaspoon ground oregano
3 cups tomato juice

In 2-quart casserole, place the chicken breasts, meaty side up. Sprinkle with garlic and oregano. Pour tomato juice over chicken and cover. Cook on Medium for 40 minutes. Rearrange chicken. Cook on Medium for another 10 minutes or until chicken is done and the juice thickened. Makes 6 servings.

Meatball Soup

Reheat in a mug for a quick, low-calorie meal.

2 lbs. lean ground beef or ground veal
1 (46-oz.) can tomato juice
2 (8-oz.) cans tomato sauce
1/2 teaspoon oregano
1/2 teaspoon salt
1/4 teaspoon pepper
2 tablespoons instant minced onion

1 tablespoon garlic powder
1 tablespoon Worcestershire sauce
2 cups diced carrots
2 cups diced celery
1 cup diced zucchini
1 cup sliced fresh mushrooms

Form meat into walnut-size meatballs. Place in 3-quart shallow casserole. Cook on High for 8 minutes. Rearrange the meat in the dish carefully so the meatballs will not be broken. Drain fat and set aside. In 4-1/2-quart bowl, combine tomato juice, tomato sauce and all the spices. Bring to a boil on High. Add the carrots, celery and zucchini. Cover. Cook on High for 10 minutes or until soft. Add the mushrooms and cover. Cook on High for 5 minutes. Add the meat to the tomato-vegetable mixture. Cover. Heat on High to serving temperature. Makes 8 servings.

Shrimp Sauté with Bean Sprouts

Delicate shrimp flavor with seasonings from the Far East.

1 tablespoon olive oil
1 lb. green shrimp, shelled and deveined
   (washed and drained on several layers
   of paper towels)
1 garlic clove, minced
1 tablespoon finely minced chives

1/2 teaspoon ground ginger
1/2 cup water
1-1/2 tablespoons instant chicken bouillon
1 lb. fresh bean sprouts,
   washed and drained
2 tablespoons soy sauce

Preheat the browning dish on High for 5 minutes. Quickly add the olive oil, shrimp, garlic, chives and ginger. Stir. Cook on Medium for 1 minute. Stir. Cook 1 minute longer or until shrimp are pink. In a 2-quart casserole make chicken broth by bringing to a boil the water and instant chicken-bouillon, about 1-1/2 minutes on High. Add the drained bean sprouts. Cover. Cook on Medium for 4-1/2 minutes. Add the bean sprouts and soy sauce to the shrimp. Cover. Cook on Medium for 1 minute. Makes 4 servings.

Sweets

This recipe group includes cakes and frostings, pie crusts and fillings, cookies and brownies, candy, dessert toppings, puddings and applesauce.

Microwave-prepared desserts are so convenient! With some advance preparation, the desserts cook while you pour the coffee. Cupcakes bake in 4 minutes, Cherry Cobbler and Baked Custard in about 10 minutes. There's something special about fresh-from-the-oven desserts.

Cakes cooked in a microwave may be moist on top. Use the Browner for 2 to 3 minutes and the cake will look better and be easier to frost. Don't use vegetable oil or non-stick spray.

Cake mixes rise higher in a microwave. Fill cake dishes no more than half full. Use extra batter for cupcakes.

Cake mixes require 4 minutes of mixing with a portable mixer on medium speed. Let the batter stand in the baking dish for 5 minutes before baking.

See Packaged Cake-Mix Table and Crumb Crusts, page 174.

Fresh Strawberry Pie

A delightful fresh-fruit dessert.

5 pints fresh strawberries
1 cup sugar
1/4 cup cornstarch
3/4 cup water

1 tablespoon lemon juice or
   Grand Marnier liqueur
1 tablespoon red JELL-O®
Pastry for One-Crust Pie, page 161

Wash berries; set aside one rounded cup of the "less-than-perfect" berries. Let remaining berries dry on paper toweling. Blend sugar and cornstarch. Puree in blender the cup of set-aside berries. Add the sugar-cornstarch mixture and water to the berry puree and blend together. Pour into a 4-cup glass measure. Cook on High for 4 to 5 minutes or until clear. Stir once. Add lemon juice or liqueur and JELL-O® to enhance color. Cool to lukewarm. Brush the baked pie crust with some of the glaze. Toss the remaining berries gently in the rest of the glaze and pour into crust. Chill. Makes one 9-inch pie.

German Chocolate Cake

A continental bakery delight.

1 (4-oz.) bar sweet cooking chocolate	1 teaspoon vanilla
1/3 cup water	1-3/4 cups flour
1/2 cup butter	1 teaspoon baking soda
1 cup sugar	1/2 teaspoon salt
3 eggs	2/3 cup buttermilk

Combine chocolate with water in 2-cup measure. Cook on High for 2 minutes, stirring several times; cool. Cream butter. Gradually add sugar, creaming until light. Add eggs, one at a time, beating well after each. Blend in vanilla and chocolate mixture. Sift together dry ingredients. Add to creamed mixture, alternately with buttermilk, beating after each addition. Line bottom of two 8-1/4-inch baking dishes with two layers of wax paper. Pour in batter. Let stand 15 minutes. Cook, one layer at a time, on Medium for 7 minutes. Brown 3 to 4 minutes. Cool 5 minutes. Turn out on cooling rack. Makes one 8-1/4-inch layer cake.

Old-Fashioned Carrot Cake

A moist and nutty cake.

1-1/2 cups sugar	2-1/2 teaspoons cinnamon
1 cup oil	1-1/4 teaspoons soda
1 teaspoon vanilla	2-1/4 cups grated raw carrots
3 eggs	1/2 cup chopped walnuts
1-1/2 cups unsifted flour	1/2 cup raisins
3/4 teaspoon salt	

In a large mixing bowl, mix sugar, oil and vanilla. Add eggs; beat well. Combine flour, salt, cinnamon and soda. Stir into egg mixture. Fold in carrots, walnuts and raisins. Pour batter into 12" x 7" baking dish which has been greased on bottom only. Cook on High for 14 to 16 minutes, giving dish one-half turn every 4 minutes. Cool. Frost with Cream-Cheese Frosting, page 159. Makes one cake.

Double-Duty Cake Mix

As delicious as it is efficient.

1 pkg. cake mix (yellow, white, spice or chocolate)	2 eggs
	1-1/3 or 1-1/2 cups water

Pour cake mix into mixing bowl; add eggs and water. Beat with electric mixer on medium speed for 4 minutes. Fill 6 paper-lined custard cups half full. Oil bottom of 7-1/2" x 12" utility dish. Pour remainder of batter into dish. Bake cupcakes on Medium for 4 minutes. Remove from oven. Bake rectangular cake on Medium for 11 to 13 minutes. Brown for 3 to 4 minutes. Cool. Top with Brown 'n Serve Peanut-Butter Frosting, page 159. Makes 6 cupcakes and one 7-1/2" x 12" cake.

German-Chocolate-Cake Frosting

Traditional frosting with new richness.

1 cup evaporated milk
1 cup sugar
3 egg yolks, slightly beaten
1/4 cup butter or margarine

1 teaspoon vanilla
1-1/3 cups flaked coconut
1 cup chopped pecans

In deep 2-quart glass bowl, combine milk, sugar, egg yolks, butter or margarine and vanilla. Cook on Medium for 5 minutes. Cool. Beat until thick and shiny. Stir in coconut and pecans. Spread between layers and on top of cake. Makes frosting for two 8-1/4-inch layer cakes.

Cream-Cheese Frosting

Rich—but not too sweet.

1/2 lb. powdered sugar
1 (3-oz.) pkg. cream cheese

3 tablespoons butter
1 teaspoon vanilla

Place sugar in 2-quart casserole. Add cream cheese, butter and vanilla. Cook on High for 1 minute, just until ingredients can be beaten together. Beat with electric mixer until fluffy. Makes enough to frost 7"x12" cake.

Brown 'n Serve Peanut-Butter Frosting

A tasty delight for all ages.

1/3 cup peanut butter
1/3 cup light cream
1 cup brown sugar, firmly packed

1 (7-1/2" x 12") baked yellow
    or chocolate cake

Mix peanut butter with cream and sugar. Spoon onto cooled cake. Raise shelf and brown 4 to 5 minutes, turning dish once. Frosting should be bubbly and slightly brown. Makes enough frosting for one 7-1/2" x 12" cake.

Seven-Minute Frosting

An old favorite made with a new trick.

1-1/2-cups sugar
1/4 teaspoon cream of tartar

6 tablespoons water
3 egg whites

In 1-quart measuring cup, cook sugar, cream of tartar and water on High for 4-1/2 minutes. Stir after 2 minutes of cooking time. Beat 3 egg whites to the soft-peak stage. Slowly add the syrup, with mixer on high speed, until icing is thick. If icing gets too thick and has a tendency to break or crumble, cook on High for 10 seconds to soften. Makes frosting for an 8-inch, 2-layer cake.

Blackbottom Pie

This rich pie is requested again and again.

1/4 cup water
2 (1-oz.) squares unsweetened chocolate
2 cups (1pt.) half and half
4 eggs, separated
1/2 cup sugar
3 tablespoons cornstarch
2 teaspoons vanilla
2 tablespoons milk

1 tablespoon unflavored gelatin
 (1 envelope)
2 teaspoons rum or rum extract
1/8 teaspoon cream of tartar
1/4 cup sugar
Pastry for One-Crust Pie (see recipe below)
Sweetened whipped cream
Chocolate shavings

In 2-cup liquid measure, combine water and chocolate. Melt on Medium for 1 to 2 minutes, stirring until chocolate is completely melted. Set aside. In 2-cup liquid measure, heat half and half on High for 1-1/2 to 2-1/2 minutes or until hot. In a 1-1/2 quart casserole, beat egg yolks with a wire wisk. Blend in hot half and half. Combine sugar and cornstarch; blend into egg-milk mixture. Cook on High for 2 minutes. Stir. Continue to cook on High for 2 to 3 minutes, stirring every 1/2 minute until thickened. Stir in vanilla. Remove 1 cup of pudding mixture and blend into chocolate. Pour into bottom of pie shell. Chill. Combine milk and gelatin in custard cup. Dissolve gelatin on High for 15 to 20 seconds. Stir to blend, then stir into remaining vanilla pudding. Flavor with rum or extract. Beat egg whites and cream of tartar until frothy. Slowly beat in sugar. Beat until stiff peaks form. Stir rum-flavored pudding or beat lightly with mixer if necessary to smooth. Fold in egg whites and spoon over chocolate filling. Chill. Top with sweetened whipped cream and chocolate shavings. Makes 8 to 10 servings.

Variations:
Use graham-cracker crust, gingersnap crust or chocolate-cookie crust for pie shell.

Pastry for One-Crust Pie

A flaky crust with rich color.

1-1/2 cups flour
3/4 teaspoon salt

1/2 cup shortening
3 to 4 tablespoons cold water

Mix together the flour and salt. Using a pastry blender, cut in the shortening until mixture resembles coarse meal. Sprinkle the water over the mixture, a tablespoon at a time. Ingredients should form a soft workable ball of dough. Gather dough together with a light touch. Shape into a ball. Let ball of dough stand about 5 minutes before rolling into a shell. Shape ball of dough into flat circle, being careful to eliminate all cracks at edge of dough. Roll into circle 1/8" thick, large enough to fit a 9-inch pie plate. Flour the rolling pin slightly and roll dough on pin. Carefully unroll dough into pie plate. Make certain dough is not stretched and fits well into plate. The edge must be built up above the edge of plate and fluted. Prick dough thoroughly. Bake on Medium for 7 to 9 minutes, giving dish a quarter turn after 3 minutes. Place shelf in upper position. Brown 2-1/2 to 3 minutes. Makes one 9-inch crust.

Blackbottom Pie

Grasshopper Pie

A velvety dessert for special occasions.

1/4 cup butter
16 to 18 chocolate cookies with
   vanilla-creme filling, crushed
35 large marshmallows
   (about 8 oz.)
1/2 cup milk

1/4 cup green creme de menthe
1/4 cup white creme de cacao
1 cup whipping cream
Whipping cream for garnish
Chocolate curls

In 9-inch pie plate, melt butter on High for 40 seconds. Add crushed cookies and mix well. Press mixture into bottom and sides of pie plate to form shell. Cook on High for 1-1/2 to 2 minutes. Set aside and cool. In 2-quart bowl, heat marshmallows and milk on High for 2- to 2-1/2 minutes or until marshmallows are puffy and begin to melt. Stir well until marshmallows are completely melted. Cool several minutes. Stir in liqueurs. Cool until partially thickened. Whip cream; fold into marshmallow mixture. Spoon into cookie-lined pie plate. Refrigerate until firm. Garnish with additional whipped cream and chocolate curls if desired. Makes 6 to 8 servings.

Elegant Bread Pudding

The sweet tang of marmalade adds to this surprise pudding.

2 cups milk
1 tablespoon butter or margarine
3 eggs
1/2 cup sugar
1/4 teaspoon salt

1 teaspoon vanilla
3/4 teaspoon cinnamon
1/3 cup chopped nuts
3 cups soft raisin-bread cubes
1/2 cup orange marmalade

Meringue:
3 egg whites
6 tablespoons sugar

1/8 teaspoon salt

In 4-cup glass measure, heat milk and butter or margarine on High for 4-1/2 minutes. Beat eggs, blend in sugar. Gradually add hot milk to eggs; stir until well blended. Stir in salt, vanilla, cinnamon and nuts. Place bread cubes in 7-1/2" x 12" baking dish. Pour egg mixture over bread. Cook on Medium for 3 to 4 minutes. Turn dish. Cook 3 to 4 minutes more. Raise shelf. Brown for 4 to 5 minutes. Spread orange marmalade over cooked pudding. Top with meringue. Brown 3 to 4 minutes.

Meringue:
Beat egg whites with salt until frothy. Gradually beat in sugar. Beat until stiff and glossy.

Autumn Apple Pie

Fresh apples with cheese-crumb topping.

6 tart cooking apples
1 cup sugar
2 tablespoons flour
1 teaspoon ground cinnamon

1 teaspoon grated lemon peel
1/8 teaspoon cloves
1/8 teaspoon salt
Pie Crust for Autumn Apple Pie (see below)

Cheese-Crumb Topping:
1/4 cup butter, melted
1/2 cup flour
1/2 cup grated Cheddar cheese

1/4 cup sugar
1/8 teaspoon salt
Sour cream

Peel, quarter and core apples; slice thinly. Toss the slices lightly with a mixture of the sugar, flour, cinnamon, lemon peel, cloves and salt. Arrange the apples, overlapping the slices, in Pie Crust for Autumn Apple Pie (see below). With shelf in upper position, cook on High for 9 minutes.

Topping:
Melt butter in 1-cup glass measure on High for 40 seconds. Add flour, cheese, sugar and salt. Mix well. Sprinkle the cheese crumbs over the apples, gently blending crumbs with a knife. Cook on High for 1 minute. Brown for 5 minutes or until golden brown. Let the pie cool on a wire rack and serve it warm, topping each slice with a generous spoonful of sour cream. Makes 8 servings.

Pie Crust for Autumn Apple Pie

Flaky pie crust with the subtle flavor of sour cream.

1-1/2 cups flour
3/4 teaspoon salt
1/2 cup shortening, colored with
　　yellow food coloring

3 to 4 tablespoons dairy sour cream

Follow instructions for Pastry for One-Crust Pie, page 161, substituting sour cream for water. Prick pastry thoroughly, but lightly, to prevent puffing during baking. Move shelf to upper position. Cook on Medium for 7 to 9 minutes, giving dish a quarter turn after 4 minutes. Brown 2-1/2 to 3-1/2 minutes. Makes 1 pie crust.

Creamy Cheese Pie

Cheese pie lovers rejoice!

Crust:
1 cup graham-cracker crumbs
1/4 cup melted butter or margarine

Filling:

2 eggs, well beaten
1 (8-oz.) pkg. cream cheese, softened
1/2 cup sugar
1/8 teaspoon salt

1 teaspoon vanilla
1/8 teaspoon almond flavoring
1-1/2 cups dairy sour cream
Cinnamon

Crust:

Mix crumbs and butter. Press on side and bottom of pie plate. Cook on High 1-1/2 to 2 minutes.

Filling:

In mixing bowl, combine eggs with cream cheese, sugar, salt, vanilla and almond flavoring. Beat until smooth. Stir in sour cream. Cook on Low for 10 minutes, stirring every 2 minutes. Pour into baked crumb crust. Cook cheesecake on Low for 3 minutes. Rotate dish a quarter turn and continue cooking 1 to 3 minutes or until center is set. Chill several hours before serving. Serve plain, or sprinkle with cinnamon, or top with prepared fruit-pie filling. Makes 6 to 8 servings.

Jubilee Cherry Topping

The perfect complement for Creamy Cheese Pie.

1 (1-lb.) can pitted sour cherries
1/4 cup reserved cherry water
1-1/4 cups Burgundy or rosé wine
1 (4-3/4-oz.) pkg. raspberry-currant
   or strawberry Danish-Dessert mix

1/4 cup sugar
1/8 teaspoon cinnamon
1/8 teaspoon nutmeg
1/2 teaspoon almond extract

Drain cherries, reserving 1/4 cup cherry water. Combine cherry water, wine, Danish-Dessert mix and sugar in a 1-1/2 quart casserole. Mix thoroughly. Bring to a boil on High for 4 to 5 minutes until thick and clear, stirring occasionally. Stir in remaining ingredients. Cover surface with a film of wax paper or plastic wrap. Chill. Makes topping for 1 cheese pie.

Variation:

Substitute pitted Bing cherries for a great flavor contrast. Substitute cherry syrup for cherry water and delete sugar.

 *Tip* *Remove freezer paper easily from a frozen package after heating on High for 15 seconds. Let stand for 2 to 3 minutes.*

Baked Custard

Soft, smooth and unbelievably easy.

2 cups milk
3 eggs, slightly beaten
1/4 cup sugar

1/2 teaspoon vanilla
Nutmeg

In 4-cup glass measure, heat milk on High for 3 minutes. Add eggs, sugar and vanilla with rotary beater. Pour into five 6-ounce custard cups. Sprinkle with nutmeg. Arrange in circle 1 inch apart. Cook on Low for 5 minutes. Rearrange custard cups on shelf; let stand for 45 seconds. Cook on Medium for 4 minutes longer or until custard starts to bubble. Cool. Makes 5 servings.

Peach Melba

Serve this in tall stemware for a colorful treat.

1 pkg. frozen raspberries
1/2 cup currant jelly
2 tablespoons cornstarch

2 tablespoons water
6 canned peach halves
Vanilla ice cream

Place the raspberries in 1-1/2-quart glass bowl. Thaw on Medium for 3 minutes. Mash berries with a spoon. Sieve to separate the seeds. Add the jelly and bring just to a boil. Add the cornstarch mixed with water and cook on High until clear and mixture thickens, stirring often with wire wisk. Chill. Place a canned peach half, cut side up, in each individual dessert dish. Top each with a scoop of ice cream and pour the cooled sauce over the top. Makes 6 servings.

Bananas Foster

Elegant and easy.

2 tablespoons butter or margarine
2 firm bananas (with slightly green tips)
1 teaspoon lemon juice

1/4 cup brown sugar, firmly packed
1/8 teaspoon rum flavoring or
  1 tablespoon rum

In 8-inch round baking dish, melt butter or margarine on High for 30 seconds. Cut bananas lengthwise in half, then crosswise in half. Place, cut side down, in melted butter. Sprinkle with lemon juice, then brown sugar and rum. Cook on High for 30 seconds. Turn dish. Cook another 30 to 45 seconds. Serve warm over vanilla or butter-pecan ice cream. Makes 4 servings.

Chunky Applesauce

Tastes like fresh-picked apples.

6 cooking apples
1/3 cup sugar

Peel and core apples. Cut into small chunks. Place in 2-quart casserole. Cover. Cook on High for 8 minutes, stirring several times. Add sugar. Cook on High an additional 2 minutes. Let stand, covered, for 5 minutes. Cool. Sprinkle with nutmeg or cinnamon, if desired. Makes about 2 cups.

Cherry Cobbler

Sweet fruit filling with crumbly topping.

1 (21-oz.) can prepared cherry-pie filling
3/4 cup flour
2 tablespoons sugar
1 teaspoon baking powder
1/8 teaspoon salt

3 tablespoons butter
  softened
2 tablespoons milk
1 egg, slightly beaten

Pour pie filling into 8-1/4-inch, shallow, round baking dish. Combine flour with sugar, baking powder and salt. Cut in butter until mixture resembles coarse crumbs. Mix milk with egg. Add to dry mixture, stirring just to moisten. Spoon topping over fruit in 5 mounds. Cook on Medium for 6 minutes, turning baking dish several times. Brown for 4 to 5 minutes. Makes 5 servings.

Pineapple Upside-Down Cake

Always a favorite and needs no frosting!

2 tablespoons butter or margarine
1/2 cup brown sugar, firmly packed
5 slices pineapple with syrup

5 maraschino cherries
1 (18-1/2-oz.) pkg. yellow cake mix.

Melt butter or margarine on High for 30 seconds in 8-1/4-inch round or 8-inch square dish. Stir in brown sugar. Drain pineapple, reserving syrup. Arrange pineapple slices and cherries over brown sugar. Prepare cake mix according to package directions, substituting pineapple syrup for water. Spoon 1/2 of batter over pineapple. Use the other 1/2 of batter for another upside-down cake or cupcakes. Cook on Medium for 8 to 9 minutes, turning dish several times. Brown 3 to 4 minutes. Let stand 1 minute. Turn upside down on cake plate. Serve warm or cold. Makes 5 to 6 servings.

Peach Soufflé

A beautiful dessert, fit for a king.

2 cups hot water
1 (3-oz.) pkg. orange-flavored gelatin
1 (3-oz.) pkg. peach-flavored gelatin
2 (10 to 12-oz.) pkgs. frozen peaches
   in syrup

1-1/4 cups syrup drained from peaches;
   add water if necessary
1 (8-oz.) pkg. cream cheese
2 cups (1 pt.) whipping cream

In 2-1/2-quart casserole bring hot water to a boil on High for 4 to 5 minutes. Add gelatins, stirring to dissolve. Refrigerate. Remove frozen peaches from cardboard-metal containers, or snip plastic pouches and place in a glass bowl. Defrost on Medium for 3 to 4 minutes or until peaches can be broken apart. Stir once while defrosting. Drain syrup and reserve. Save some peaches for the top and chop remaining peaches into bite-size pieces. Remove cream cheese from foil wrapper and place in small mixing bowl. Soften on Low for 1 to 1-1/2 minutes. Beat with an electric mixer. Gradually blend in peach syrup. Stir into gelatin mixture. Refrigerate until gelatin mounds (about 2 hours). Whip cream. Two cups cream will make 4 cups whipped cream. Reserve 1 cup whipped cream. Fold peaches and the other 3 cups whipped cream into gelatin. Pour into 6 individual soufflé dishes with 1/2-inch collars or one 5 to 6-cup soufflé dish with a 2-inch collar. Garnish with reserved peach slices and reserved cup of whipped cream. Makes 6 servings.

Baked Apples

A tasty dessert and a breakfast treat, too.

4 medium cooking apples
4 tablespoons brown sugar

2 tablespoons butter
Dash cinnamon or nutmeg

Core apples. Cut a strip of peel from the top of each. Place apples in 8-inch round cake dish. Press 1 tablespoon brown sugar into each hole. Add 1/2 teaspoon butter and a dash of cinnamon or nutmeg. Cook apples on Low for 5 minutes. Turn dish. Cook on Medium for 5 minutes. Place apples in serving dish. Pour any syrup left in the baking dish into the center of apples. Cool before serving. Makes 4 servings.

Peach Soufflé

Tip   *Heat brandy for flaming foods on High for 15 seconds. Ignite and pour over food.*

Thermatronic Fudge

For chocolate lovers of all ages.

1 lb. powdered sugar, sifted
1/2 cup cocoa
1/4 cup milk

1/4 lb. butter or margarine
1 tablespoon vanilla
1/2 cup nuts

Line and 8" x 8" glass baking dish with waxed paper. Blend sugar and cocoa in a 2-quart mixing bowl and add milk and butter or margarine. Cook on High for 1 minute 45 seconds. Remove bowl from oven and beat until smooth. Add vanilla and nuts and stir until blended. Pour fudge into paper-lined baking dish. Refrigerate until firm. To serve, run a knife along the edge of the baking dish. Turn upside down on a plate. Remove wax paper. Place right side up on a cutting board and cut as desired. Makes 36 small pieces.

Variations:

For Mint Fudge, prepare as above and add several drops peppermint extract.

For Rocky Variation, prepare as above but increase milk from 1/4 to 1/3 cup. When adding vanilla and nuts, include a rounded cup of miniature marshmallows and 1/8 teaspoon peppermint extract, if desired. Marshmallows will retain their shape if they are frozen ahead of time.

Quick Hot-Fudge Sauce

Satisfies that craving for something yummy.

1/3 cup milk
1 (6-oz.) pkg. semi-sweet chocolate chips

Combine milk and chocolate chips in 4-cup measure. Heat on High 2 to 3 minutes. Stir. Serve hot. Makes 4 servings.

Praline Cookies

So easy your children can make them.

8 graham crackers
1/3 cup chopped pecans

4 tablespoons (1/2 stick) of margarine
1/2 cup brown sugar, firmly packed

Break 8 crackers in half and place 4 halves across and 4 down in 8" x 8" glass baking dish. Sprinkle the chopped nuts evenly over the crackers. In 4-cup measure, combine margarine and brown sugar. Cook on High for 1-1/2 minutes. Stir well and pour over the crackers. Cook on Low for 2-1/2 minutes. Raise shelf. Brown for 3 minutes. Spread evenly over the crackers. After the cookies are cool, cut them apart. Makes 16 cookies.

Brownies

These do a fast disappearing act.

2/3 cup butter or margarine
1 cup sugar
2 eggs, slightly beaten
1 teaspoon vanilla
1 cup sifted all-purpose flour

1/4 cup dry cocoa
1/4 cup instant cocoa
1/2 teaspoon baking powder
1/2 cup chopped walnuts

Melt butter or margarine in bowl on High for 1 minute or until melted. Add sugar. Cool. Add eggs and vanilla. Sift flour, dry cocoa, instant cocoa and baking powder into sugar mixture and blend in. Stir in nuts. Pour into lightly greased 9-inch glass pie plate. Cook on High for 4-1/2 to 5-1/2 minutes, turning 3 times. Cool before cutting. Makes 1 dozen brownies.

Chewy Nut-Bars

A cake full of surprises!

3 tablespoons butter
1/2 cup flour
1/4 teaspoon baking soda
1/8 teaspoon salt
1-1/2 cups brown sugar, firmly packed

1-1/2 cups finely chopped walnuts
3 eggs, beaten
1-1/2 teaspoon vanilla
Powdered sugar

In 7-1/2" x 12" baking dish, melt butter on High for 35 seconds. In mixing bowl, combine flour, baking soda, salt, brown sugar and nuts. Stir in eggs and vanilla. Carefully pour batter over melted butter in baking dish. Do not stir. Raise shelf. Cook on Medium for 7 minutes. Turn dish. Cook another 7 minutes. Brown for 3 to 4 minutes, turning dish at the end of 2 minutes. Remove from oven and cut into 24 bars. When completely cool, remove bars to cooling rack. Sprinkle with powdered sugar. Makes 24 bars.

Quick Peach Brûlée

A quick, low-calorie variation of a traditional favorite.

2 fresh peaches, peeled and halved
    or 4 canned peach halves, drained
3/4 cup dairy sour cream

1 tablespoon granulated sugar
1/4 teaspoon grated lemon peel
3/4 cup brown sugar, firmly packed

Arrange peach halves, cut side down, in 4 custard cups. Cook on High for 1 minute. Combine sour cream with granulated sugar and lemon peel. Spoon over fruit. Just before serving, sprinkle brown sugar over entire surface of sour cream. Raise shelf. Brown for 3 to 3-1/2 minutes or until brown sugar begins to melt. Serve immediately. Makes 4 servings.

Divinity

Mounds of sugar-spun sweetness.

3 cups granulated sugar
1/2 cup light corn syrup
2/3 cup water
1/4 teaspoon salt

2 egg whites
1/4 teaspoon vanilla
1 cup chopped nuts

In 3-quart bowl, cook sugar, syrup and water on High for 12 to 13 minutes until it spins a fine thread. Add salt to egg whites and beat them on high speed until stiff. Slowly pour syrup mixture in a thin stream into the egg whites, beating constantly until mixture loses its shine and thickens. Stir in vanilla and nuts. Drop by teaspoons at once on waxed paper. Makes about 30 pieces.

Merry Mints

Something special for the holidays.

3 tablespoons butter or margarine
3 tablespoons milk
1 (15.4-oz.) pkg. creamy white-frosting mix

1/2 teaspoon peppermint extract
Food coloring

In 1-1/2-quart bowl, heat butter or margarine and milk until butter or margarine melts. Stir in frosting mix. Cook on High for 1-1/2 to 2 minutes or until bubbly. Stir often. Add peppermint and desired food coloring. Drop from spoon on waxed paper. Makes about 4 dozen mints.

Fantastic Fudge

Rich chocolate—laced with marshmallow creme.

4 cups sugar
1 (14-oz.) can evaporated milk
1 cup butter or margarine
1 (12-oz.) pkg. semi-sweet chocolate pieces

1 (7-oz.) jar marshmallow creme
1 teaspoon vanilla
1 cup chopped walnuts

In 4-quart bowl, combine sugar, milk and butter or margarine. Cook on High for 18 to 20 minutes or until mixture reaches soft-ball stage. Stir often while mixture is cooking. Watch carefully to avoid boiling over. Mix in chocolate and marshmallow creme. Stir until well blended. Add vanilla and nuts. Pour into buttered 9-inch square dish for thick pieces. For thinner pieces, use 7-1/2" x 12" dish. Cool and cut into squares. Makes about 20 pieces.

Top to bottom: Merry Mints, Divinity, Fantastic Fudge.

Packaged Cake-Mix Baking Table

TYPE	UTENSIL	TIME AND POWER LEVEL	PROCEDURE
Cake Mix (18-1/2-oz.)			Reduce liquid indicated on package by 1/4 cup. Fill utensil or cups only half full of batter.
Cupcakes 2 4 6	6-oz. custard cups or microwave cupcake utensil	Medium for 2-1/2 to 2-1/2 minutes Medium for 3 to 3-1/2 minutes Medium for 4 to 5 minutes	Use cupcake papers inside utensil. Place shelf in lower position. Remove cupcakes from utensil immediately after cooking.
Layer Cake 1 layer	8-inch round cake dish	Medium for 6-1/2 to 7 minutes. Cool 10 minutes before turning out of dish.	Grease only bottom of dish. Reduce liquid as above. Fill dish half full and use remaining batter for 2 extra cupcakes. Place shelf in lower position.
Sheet Cake	7-1/2"x12" utility dish	Medium for 11 to 12 minutes. Cool 10 minutes before turning out of dish.	Same as for layer cake. Remaining batter makes 6 cupcakes. Place shelf in lower position.
Gingerbread (14-oz.)	8-inch square dish	High for 7-1/2 to 8-1/2 minutes. Cool 15 minutes before turning out of dish.	Grease only bottom of dish. Use all batter. Place shelf in upper position.
Snackin' Cake® (14-1/2-oz.)	8-inch round dish	High for 7 to 8 minutes Cool 10 minutes before turning out of dish.	Use all batter. Place shelf in lower position.

Crumb Crusts for 9-inch Pie

	INGREDIENTS	COOKING TIME
Graham Cracker Crust (18 to 20 squares)	6 tablespoons butter Combine: 1-1/2 cup crumbs, 1/4 cup sugar	Place shelf in upper position. Heat for 1-1/2 to 2 minutes. Brown 3 minutes.
Cookie or Wafer Crust	6 tablespoons butter 1-1/2 cup crumbs	Place shelf in upper position. Heat on High for 1-1/2 to 2 minutes. Brown 2-1/2 minutes.

Melt butter in pie plate, on High for about 30 to 45 seconds. Add crumbs. Press mixture evenly to bottom and sides of plate. Cook, turning twice. Brown as desired.

Index

9.9.97481321624